The
Vegan Cookie
Connoisseur

The Vegan Cookie Connoisseur

Over 140 Simply Delectable Vegan Recipes
That Treat the Eyes and Taste Buds

Kelly Peloza

Skyhorse Publishing

Skyhorse Publishing books may be purchased in bulk at special discounts for sales promotion, corporate gifts, fund-raising, or educational purposes. Special editions can also be created to specifications. For details, contact the Special Sales Department, Skyhorse Publishing, 307 West 36th Street, 11th Floor, New York, NY 10018 or info@skyhorsepublishing.com.

www.skyhorsepublishing.com

10 9 8 7 6 5 4 3 2

Library of Congress Cataloging-in-Publication Data

Peloza, Kelly.
   The vegan cookie connoisseur : over 140 simply delectable vegan recipes that treat the eyes and taste buds / Kelly Peloza.
      p. cm.
   Includes bibliographical references and index.
   ISBN 978-1-61608-121-8 (alk. paper)
   1. Cookies. 2. Vegan cookery. I. Title.
   TX772.P37 2010
   641.5'636--dc22
                              2010021477

Printed in China

Contents

Acknowledgments

To all my friends and family, taste testers, herbivores, cookie lovers, and everyone who encouraged me to bake endlessly.

Special thanks to . . .

Erica Mendoza, who tested about 100 recipes, for contributing so much to the creation of this book.

Katie Hubbard of Don't Eat Off the Sidewalk! for being awesome and letting me crash on her Internet couch.

Drake, for taste testing a few recipes, especially the dog treats.

Garrick Stegner, for donating a few recipes and helping out along the way.

Louzilla Ryan, for always being eager to proofread and test, and being all-around fantastic!

All my testers. I never could have done this without your ideas, reassurance, and constructive criticism. Thank you!

Erica and Daniel Mendoza	Melisser Elliott	Nicole Carpenter
Tami Noyes	Jennifer Albaum	Joan Farkas
Caitlin Johnson	Jen Briselli	Diana Harman
Elizabeth Ryan	Stephanie Roy	Melissa Tsang
Carmen Borsa	Jen M.	Carrie Lynn Morse
Ditte Johansen	Evan McGraw	Sarah Baker
Nicole Assumpcao	Laura Swan	Ashley Stephen
Brooke Osborne	Nicole Carnes	Jasmine Phair
Lindsey Osterloh	Sarah Keeler	Kristen Miano
Catherine Dunleavy	Kayla K.	Nadine Doupe
Thalia C. Palmer	Kathryn Diogo	Jennifer Hamilton
Jillian Balinski	Madeline Sherrill	Céline Land

Introduction

I remember the moment perfectly. Several years ago at Christmastime, I was making gingerbread people when inspiration struck. I would write a book entirely devoted to vegan cookies! At first it was just a pipe dream, but the more I sat on the idea, the more I knew I had to make it become a reality. I started writing this book during the summer of 2007 as a high school student soon to be a cookie-making machine. Creating and perfecting more than 140 recipes did have its challenges, but making vegan versions of old favorites and creating brand-new cookies people could enjoy for years to come was an immensely valuable experience.

My objective for this project was to create a comprehensive collection of cookie recipes while staying true to my belief that vegan baking needn't be inaccessible or anything less than delicious. Immense dedication was put into the creation of every recipe in order to make each one unique, and because I'm a firm believer that seeing is at least half of tasting, I wanted to be sure all the recipes were accompanied by mouthwatering photos to guide and inspire you. Each recipe is tried and true due to extensive evaluations from my recipe testers (and taste testers!). These recipes are for anyone—people new to baking, experienced culinary connoisseurs, vegans and nonvegans alike.

You'll find only affordable, accessible ingredients in these cookies. One problem many people run across when they're new to vegan baking is that so many recipes call for obscure ingredients, such as soy milk powder or silken tofu. Making a batch of chocolate chip cookies shouldn't involve running to five different health food stores searching for some elusive ingredient. And egg replacer? Animal-free baking is about making delicious dairy-free, egg-free desserts that don't need eggs, nor a special commercial ingredient to replace them. But more on that later.

Why *The Vegan Cookie Connoisseur*? Vegan cookies are impressive, and the best part is that you don't need fancy kitchen equipment or exotic ingredients to create these elegant desserts in your own home. Anyone with the will and a little patience can be a cookie connoisseur!

My dream was to share my recipes with the world and, ridiculous amounts of sugar and 500 batches of cookies later, I have a concrete way to do just that. Whether you follow the cookie recipes to a T or use them as a base for your own creations, I hope you enjoy using the recipes as much as I loved writing them. Bake cookies for yourself, your family, your friends, your coworkers, or anyone whose day you want to brighten!

Thank you for joining in and spreading the cookie love. Everyone should know how amazing vegan baking can be!

How to Be a Cookie Connoisseur

Ingredients

Every cookie connoisseur should have a well-stocked kitchen—you never know when you'll need to whip up a batch of cookies on the spot. Here's a basic grocery list for the recipes in this book that won't break the bank or send you on a desperate ingredient scavenger hunt.

THE ABSOLUTE ESSENTIALS:

Flour: When a recipe calls for flour, it means your average unbleached all-purpose flour found in any grocery store baking aisle. Flour is a staple for cookie baking, so stock up. If you're concerned about making your cookies healthier, it's generally okay to replace half the all-purpose with whole wheat pastry flour, which can be found in many well-stocked grocery stores. This, as well as gluten-free baking, will be explained more thoroughly in chapter ten.

Sugar: Sugar is oh-so-important for creating texture and adding sweetness to cookies. Some vegans are uncomfortable using regular granulated sugar because of the filtration process. Cane sugar is sometimes processed with animal bone char; however, the char doesn't end up in the final product. If this is a concern for you, look for beet sugar, contact the company of a sugar brand and inquire about their filtration process, or use organic unrefined sugar like Florida Crystals. Don't confuse unrefined granulated sugar with turbinado sugar. The latter is much coarser and doesn't work so well for baking, although it is wonderful for sprinkling atop cookies for decoration and a little crunch.

Brown sugar: Brown sugar is just regular granulated sugar with the molasses retained, adding moisture and a deeper flavor to the sugar. I'm a big fan of brown sugar, so it shows up in my recipes a lot.

Canola oil: Oil works like butter to create a decadent texture in cookies. I use canola oil because it's accessible, cheap, and has a neutral flavor perfect for baking.

Extracts: The most common extract you'll need is pure vanilla extract. It adds a necessary depth of flavor to many baked goods. Even though it can be a little

pricey, be sure to use pure vanilla; imitation vanilla tastes very little like the real thing. Other extracts that show up in these recipes are almond, peppermint, strawberry, orange, and coconut.

Baking powder and baking soda: Without leavening agents, there would be no cookies (palatable ones, anyway). Working in different ways, baking powder and baking soda create structure in your cookies. Baking powder creates bubbles when wet and baking soda reacts with an acid to leaven the cookies. Because they work in different ways, make sure not to get the two mixed up or attempt to substitute one for the other! However, in a pinch, two parts cream of tartar and one part baking soda is an acceptable substitution for baking powder.

Salt: Salt brings out the flavors in cooking. The same principle applies to cookies and other baked goods. The amount in these recipes is very minimal once it's divided among the cookies, so worrying about the sodium or decreasing the amount of salt is unnecessary. I use sea salt for baking.

Milk: Soy, that is—my liquid of choice for baking. It's always handy to have around to add moisture to dry cookie dough. Of course you don't have to use *soy milk*. There are many varieties of nondairy milk—almond, rice, oat, hazelnut, and more. Experiment with any of these if you are allergic to soy or want to try something different. I am partial to almond milk as it has a nice subtle flavor. It should also be noted that not all brands of soy milk taste the same, so try a few different kinds to see what you like.

Nonhydrogenated margarine: Earth Balance margarine is what it's all about. It's perfect for creaming with sugar, whipping up buttercream frosting, and creating an incredibly crispy cookie. It's superb in many other applications as well, such as spreading on toast or cooking with. Margarine can be a bit pricey, especially in the large quantities required for baking, so I try to use oil more often; however, for certain recipes, margarine simply produces tastier results. Beware of margarines that contain whey or other hidden animal ingredients, and avoid margarine with hydrogenated oils.

Nonhydrogenated vegetable shortening: In addition to using it in frosting, a little bit of shortening, such as Spectrum or Earth Balance brand, added to melted chocolate will make it very smooth and luscious for dipping and coating cookies and other treats.

Chocolate chips: Vegan semisweet chocolate chips are fairly easy to find nowadays and many cheap store-brand chocolate chips just happen to be vegan. Read the labels! I like to use either Trader Joe's or Ghirardelli semisweet chocolate chips.

Other Frequently Used Ingredients:
- Liquid sweeteners: maple syrup, agave nectar, and corn syrup ("vegan" doesn't always mean "healthy"!)
- Cocoa powder • Cornstarch • Rolled oats
- Nuts and seeds
- All-natural "just peanuts" peanut butter, no salt added
- Other nut butters such as cashew and almond
- Coconut (unsweetened *and* sweetened, flaked)
- Applesauce • Citrus fruits, for their zest and juice
- Alcohol (for those fancy drinks cookies!) • Powdered sugar
- Canned pumpkin (pure pumpkin, not pumpkin pie mix)
- Raisins, dried cranberries, and other dried fruits
- Ground coffee or coffee beans • Food colorings
- Cinnamon and other baking spices
- Different flours such as spelt, oat, and rye • Dates
- Ground flaxseed

Equipment: You don't need anything particularly fancy to make spectacular cookies, but you'll want more than your bare hands. Here's a list of basic kitchen tools and appliances that range from absolutely necessary to useful to have around.
- Oven • Measuring cups • Mixing bowls • Mixing spoon
- Spatula • Cookie sheets • Parchment paper

Lining your baking sheets with parchment makes for easy cleanup. I reuse my parchment paper a few times; it'd be a waste to throw it away just because there are a few crumbs stuck to it. Some of my testers liked using reusable silicone baking mats, so consider investing in one of those for more environmentally conscious baking.

Saucepan: I'm sure you have saucepans for cooking, and you will find them useful for making the fruit sauces and caramel in this book.

Sifter: There are so many kinds of sifters to choose from. My personal favorite is the metal kind you pour the dry ingredients into, then turn the handle to sift. Alternatively, you can use a mesh strainer made for vegetables and pasta.

Electric mixer: A big stand mixer is helpful for creaming margarine and sugar, but not absolutely necessary. I do, however, advise investing in a handheld electric beater. I use mine all the time for creaming margarine and sugar for cookies, whipping up buttercream frosting, making cake batter, and more.

Sauté pan and glass dishes, important for melting chocolate (page 6).

Oven thermometer: Your oven needs to be the right temperature for accurate results! It can be shocking to realize your oven has always been several degrees off, so invest in a thermometer to keep in the know.

Oil mister: I use my oil mister all the time to spray cookie sheets with canola oil. You could just pour oil directly on the cookie sheet and spread it around, but the mister is very convenient, evenly coats the surface with just the right amount, and is affordable, so consider picking one up. It's also useful for sautéing veggies or making grilled sandwiches.

Cookie scoop: Cookie scoops are like small ice cream scoops and they have a handle you squeeze to drop batter on the cookie sheet. They're nice for precise measurements and uniform shape and size, but a regular spoon works fine, too.

Cookie cutters: I have a huge box of 100 cookie cutters I got at a craft store for ten dollars, and they were worth every penny. Start your own collection! I prefer

plastic over metal, because metal can rust and bend over time.

Food processor or mortar and pestle: My food processor is probably my favorite kitchen appliance. I use it for making hummus, grating carrots, and chopping nuts for cookies. If you don't have one, a similar effect can be achieved by placing whatever you want to crush in a plastic bag, then smashing it on a hard surface with a hammer or mallet.

How to Melt Chocolate Like a Pro

Mmm, melty chocolate. It's delicious for dipping fruit, nuts, pretzels, for drizzling atop cookies and cakes, and so much more. Many recipes in this cookbook require you to melt chocolate, so here's my official chocolate melting lesson.

The number one thing I learned about melting chocolate is to add a little bit of shortening (or oil if shortening isn't available to you). The teensiest amount makes the difference between smooth and luscious, and lumpy and unattractive.

Always temper your chocolate. That is, let it set at its own pace at room temperature. Tossing it in the freezer to harden at lightning speed may be instant gratification, but freezer-hardened chocolate will melt all over your fingers if you don't eat it all right away. Tempering will create a glossy finish, and the chocolate won't melt at room temperature. This is key when making recipes like Peanut Butter Cups (page 47).

Don't add soy milk to melted chocolate to make it smooth unless you're making ganache. Chocolate is very finicky and it will usually clump up. I'd tell you why if I was a food chemist, but I'm not, so you'll just have to take my word for it.

METHODS OF MELTING CHOCOLATE:

"Double Boiler": I don't think anyone actually owns a double boiler. And you'll never have to! Melt chocolate with ease with your makeshift double boiler. Here's how it works:

1. Get a sauté pan. 2. Fill it with water. 3. Put it over medium-high heat on the stove top. 4. Put chocolate and shortening in a glass or ceramic dish. 5. Place dish in the pan. 6. Melt that chocolate, making sure to stir often! 7. Dip!

Microwave: Put your chocolate in a microwave-safe bowl and microwave on high for about ten seconds, then stir. Microwave again, then stir. Repeat, repeat, repeat until it's melted and smooth. Doing this in increments ensures evenly melted, smooth, and nonburned chocolate.

S ome of these questions relating to baking methods and tricky ingredients come directly from the cookie testing boards and should answer some of your inquiries—perhaps even before you think to ask.

COOKIE MODUS OPERANDI:

Q: How should I measure my flour?

A: There are many different ways to measure flour, and each way will cause slight variations in measurement. When I bake, I scoop flour directly out of the container with the measuring cup, then scrape off the excess flour with my finger or a knife. Since I used that method when writing these recipes, I suggest you do that also to maintain consistency.

Q: Do I have to sift my flour?

A: Yes, unless the recipe specifies otherwise.

Q: Is it okay to halve, fourth, third, double, or triple a recipe?

A: Definitely! You can do this with almost all the recipes. The only ones I would advise against altering the quantity of are the recipes that require specific dimensions and rolling up, such as Hypnosis Cookies (page 250) and Cinnamon Roll Cookies (page 246). I halve recipes all the time to make smaller batches of several different kinds!

Q: Which rack should I bake my cookies on?

A: The middle rack will ensure even heat circulation and bake the cookies thoroughly and evenly.

Q: Can I freeze my cookie dough?
A: Yes. For specific instructions, see page 94.

Q: How should I store my cookies?
A: Store cookies in an airtight container or zip-top bag unless the recipe specifies otherwise. If any cookies need to be refrigerated, it says so in the instructions.

TROUBLESHOOTING:
Q: What should I do if my dough is dry or crumbly?
A: Adding soy milk (or another nondairy milk) will usually resolve this problem.

Q: What if my dough is too wet or liquid-y?
A: Add a couple tablespoons of flour to the dough until it holds together better.

Q: Help! Why aren't my cookies spreading?
A: Some cookies are supposed to spread and others aren't. More often than not, it's no problem if they don't.

Q: Why are my cookies undercooked on the inside?
A: You probably didn't bake them long enough and/ or your oven temperature was too high (get a thermometer!). A lower temperature and longer baking time ensures the insides have enough time to bake without burning the outsides.

Q: Why did the bottoms of my cookies burn?
A: Your oven's temperature was probably too high or they baked for too long. Check up on them before the timer goes off next time.

Q: What should I do if my cookies are crumbling?

A: Some cookies are just extremely delicate and will crumble easily, so the best thing you can do is handle them carefully. Letting these kinds of cookies sit on the tray for about five minutes after they're done baking will help prevent crumbling.

Q: Why did my cookies turn out really hard?

A: Crispy cookies can go from perfectly crispy to hard as a rock very quickly in a low-temperature oven with a long baking time, so check up on your cookies before the timer goes off.

Q: My cookies didn't turn out how they were supposed to; therefore, the recipe sucks. Does it have anything to do with the fact that I was out of flour so I swapped it for cornstarch and also only used half the oil?

A: Yes, yes it does.

INGREDIENT SPECIFICS:

Q: What kind of peanut butter should I use?

A: The default peanut butter I use is 100 percent peanuts with no salt. Any kind of "natural" peanut butter is A-OK to use. If it contains salt, just reduce the salt in the recipe a bit. It's also really helpful to store your jar of natural peanut butter upside down before opening it for the first time so the oil will be on the bottom of the jar and won't make a huge mess when you stir it.

Q: Can I use whole wheat pastry flour instead of white for the cookies? Can I use turbinado sugar? What about evaporated cane juice?

A: Yep, whole wheat pastry flour (not to be confused with regular whole wheat flour, which is far too dense) is fine to use for many of the recipes, but I recommend using a one-to-one ratio of whole wheat pastry flour to white flour, instead of using entirely whole wheat, because whole wheat tends to make the dough dry and alter the flavor. Also, there are some recipes that would be really gross with whole wheat pastry flour, like sugar cookies.

Using coarse (turbinado) sugar in place of granulated doesn't give accurate results in most situations and makes cookie dough drier. Evaporated cane juice is definitely fine to use.

Q: What kind of cocoa powder should I use? I see Dutch-process, natural, and blends of the two.
A: Natural cocoa has a strong chocolate flavor and is acidic, so it can be used to react with baking soda in recipes. Dutch-process cocoa is processed with alkali to neutralize the acidity present in natural cocoa. It's milder with a deeper, chocolaty flavor. I go for the best of both worlds and use a blend variety so it contains a bit of acidity with a mellow chocolate flavor.

Q: Is there a difference between the dark and light varieties of agave nectar?
A: The darker variety has a stronger flavor, but I use light agave nectar in the cookie recipes. Use light unless dark is specified.

Q: How long before agave goes bad?
A: It has a very long shelf life and doesn't crystallize like honey. It is just sugar, so it should last quite a long time. Don't be surprised if it's all used up before you even consider worrying about it!

The Recipes

Cookies Inspired by Drinks

From lemonade to White Russians, these sweet treats are perfect for when you want your drink in cookie form (why not?).

Glazed Apple Cider Cookies

Makes about 2 dozen

These enticing cloud-like cookies are ideal for those cool autumn months. The sweet cinnamon-y flavor and luscious soft texture accompany the colorful leaves and cool breeze perfectly.

¼ cup apple butter
½ cup apple cider
⅓ cup canola oil
¾ cup brown sugar
2 ⅔ cups flour
¾ teaspoon baking powder

⅛ teaspoon salt
2 teaspoons cinnamon
¼ teaspoon ginger
⅛ teaspoon cloves
Dash of nutmeg

For the glaze:
3 tablespoons apple cider
1 ½ cups powdered sugar
3 tablespoons brown sugar
½ teaspoon cinnamon

Preheat oven to 350°F.

In a large bowl, stir together the apple butter, apple cider, oil, and brown sugar. Sift in the flour, baking powder, salt, and spices, then stir until combined.

Drop 2 tablespoon-sized portions of dough on a greased or parchment-lined baking sheet. Bake for 9–10 minutes or until the bottoms are golden.

For the glaze: Stir all glaze ingredients together in a small bowl, then dip the cookies, let the excess glaze drip off, and let set.

Apple Cider "Donut" Variation: Before the glaze is completely set, roll the cookies in a mixture of ⅓ cup sugar, 3 tablespoons brown sugar, and 1 teaspoon cinnamon.

Chai Cookies

Makes about
2 dozen

These cookies are based on the Snickerdoodle recipe (page 230) with the addition of chai spice and black tea! This twist on an old favorite is sure to become a part of your regular baking rotation.

⅓ cup soy milk

2 chai or black tea bags

½ cup margarine

1 cup sugar

⅓ cup brown sugar

½ teaspoon vanilla extract

1 tablespoon cornstarch

2 ⅔ cups flour

¼ teaspoon salt

1 teaspoon baking powder

Spices:

1 tablespoon cinnamon

¾ teaspoon ginger

1 ½ teaspoons cardamom

½ teaspoon cloves

⅛ teaspoon ground black pepper, adjusted to personal taste

1 tablespoon coarse sugar

Preheat oven to 325°F.

Heat the soy milk in the microwave for about a minute and a half, or on the stove top until steaming hot. Add the tea bags and steep for about 10 minutes. Stir an ice cube in the tea until cool.

Cream together the margarine and sugar until fluffy. Add the vanilla, soy milk mixture, and cornstarch, and mix until incorporated. Stir together the spices in a small bowl and set aside. The spice mix should equal about 3 tablespoons. If you have premade chai spice, it's fine to use that, but you'll lose points. Sift in the flour, baking powder, salt, and 2 ½ teaspoons of the chai spice. Stir. If the dough is too dry and crumbly, add a splash of soy milk. It shouldn't be sticky, though. Mix the tablespoon of sugar with the remaining chai spice. Form the dough into 1 ½-inch balls and roll in the chai spice/sugar mixture. Place on a lightly greased cookie sheet and flatten slightly. Bake for about 12–14 minutes until golden around the edges, but still soft on top, then transfer to a wire cooling rack.

Eggnog Cookies

Makes 24 cookies

Now you can have your vegan nog in a cookie! The cookie itself is very subtle and delicate, but the glaze adds a bit of spice, complementing it perfectly.

¾ cup margarine
¼ cup canola oil
⅓ cup brown sugar
1 cup powdered sugar
1 teaspoon vanilla
2 tablespoons vegan
   eggnog or soy milk

2 tablespoons rum
2 ¼ cups flour
¼ teaspoon baking soda
¼ teaspoon baking powder
¼ teaspoon nutmeg
¼ teaspoon salt

For the glaze:
1 cup powdered sugar
1 teaspoon rum
1 tablespoon soy milk
Pinch of nutmeg

Preheat oven to 350°F.

With an electric mixer, beat the margarine, oil, sugars, and vanilla together. Add the nog and rum, then continue to mix.

Add the flour, baking powder, baking soda, nutmeg, and salt.

Drop by tablespoonfuls onto a lightly greased or parchment-lined baking sheet and bake for 9–12 minutes. Transfer to a wire rack to cool.

Meanwhile, make the glaze. Put all ingredients in a small bowl and mix. Drizzle a spoonful of glaze over each cookie when cool, let the glaze set, then eat!

Pink Lemonade Cookies

Makes about 13 sandwich cookies

If there's anything better than lemonade cookies, it's pink ones! The pink is purely for aesthetics, so you can leave it out if you must, but know that you're missing out on something akin to rainbows and fluffy puppies.

⅓ cup canola oil
⅔ cup sugar
1 tablespoon lemon zest
¼ cup soy milk
1 ⅓ cups flour

1 teaspoon baking powder
¼ teaspoon salt
Half batch of Lemon Buttercream (page 267)
Pink food coloring (optional)

Preheat oven to 350°F.

Stir together the oil and sugar until combined. Add the lemon zest and soy milk, and beat until smooth and consistent.

In a separate bowl, combine flour, baking powder, and salt. Add the dry mixture to the wet, and mix until well-combined. The dough should not be stiff.

Drop by heaping teaspoonfuls onto a baking sheet lined with parchment paper (about 2 inches apart), and flatten slightly. Bake for 9–11 minutes, or until the edges are golden brown. Let the cookies sit on the baking sheet for about a minute before transferring them to a cooling rack to cool completely.

Prepare the Lemon Buttercream and add a touch of pink food coloring if desired. Spread on the insides of half the cookies and top with the rest for sandwich cookies.

Fiesta Margarita Cookies

Makes 16–18 cookies

Margarita cookies are perfect to serve at any fiesta! Whip up a batch of these, Spicy Mexican Wedding Cookies (page 185), and Mexican Hot Chocolate Cookies (page 25) and you'll be ready to party!

3 tablespoons lime juice
½ teaspoon lime zest
¼ cup canola oil
½ cup sugar
2 ½ tablespoons turbinado sugar
3 tablespoons tequila

½ teaspoon apple cider vinegar
¼ teaspoon vanilla extract
¼ teaspoon salt
1 ¾ cups flour
½ teaspoon baking soda

Glaze:
4 teaspoons lime juice
½ teaspoon tequila
¾ cup powdered sugar
For sprinkling, mix:
1 teaspoon sugar
⅛ teaspoon salt

Preheat oven to 350°F.

In a large bowl, combine the lime juice and zest, oil, sugars, tequila, vinegar, vanilla, and salt. Stir.

Sift in the flour and baking soda, and stir until incorporated.

Flatten tablespoon-sized portions of dough on a parchment-lined or lightly greased cookie sheet and bake for about 10 minutes, or until golden around the edges. Transfer to a wire rack to cool.

Meanwhile, make the glaze. In a small bowl, stir together all ingredients. When the cookies are mostly cooled, spoon glaze atop each cookie, about ½ teaspoon of glaze each. Let sit for a few minutes (to let the glaze set a little bit, but not completely), then sprinkle on the sugar and salt mixture.

Spicy Mexican Hot Chocolate Cookies

Makes about 16 cookies

Mexican hot chocolate is a real treat! It's cinnamon-y, spicy, and chocolaty, and even more amazing when transformed into a cookie. This is one of the few times you'll add cayenne pepper to baked goods.

¼ cup coconut, rice, or soy milk
⅓ cup brown sugar
¼ cup turbinado sugar
2 tablespoons agave nectar
⅓ cup canola oil
1 teaspoon vanilla extract
⅛ teaspoon almond extract

⅛ teaspoon coconut extract
2 tablespoons powdered sugar
1 tablespoon cornmeal
1 ¼ cups flour
½ cup cocoa powder
½ teaspoon baking soda
1 teaspoon cinnamon

¼ teaspoon salt
¼ teaspoon cayenne, or to taste
For rolling:
2 teaspoons cocoa powder
1 tablespoon powdered sugar
¾ teaspoon cinnamon

Preheat oven to 350°F.

In a large bowl stir together the milk, sugars, agave, oil, extracts, powdered sugar, and cornmeal.

Combine the flour, cocoa powder, baking soda, cinnamon, and salt in a separate bowl, then sift into the wet ingredients. Add cayenne to taste.

Combine the cocoa powder, powdered sugar, and cinnamon in a small bowl.

Roll dough into tablespoon-sized balls, then roll in the mixture, coating completely. Flatten on a parchment-lined or lightly greased cookie sheet and bake for 11–12 minutes or until firm. Transfer to a wire cooling rack and sprinkle with any leftover cocoa/sugar/cinnamon mix.

Mocha Cappuccino Cookies

Makes 20 cookies

These delicacies are thin and chewy with a punch of mocha flavor and a hint of chocolate.

½ cup sugar
½ cup brown sugar
⅓ cup canola oil
¼ cup soy milk
1 teaspoon vanilla extract

2 cups flour
¼ teaspoon baking powder
¼ teaspoon baking soda
¼ teaspoon salt
2 tablespoons ground coffee
½ cup chocolate chips

Preheat oven to 350°F.

In a large bowl, mix together the sugars, oil, soy milk, and vanilla.

Add the flour, baking powder, baking soda, salt, and coffee. Stir in the chocolate chips. Add a bit more flour if the dough feels wet or a splash of soy milk if it won't hold together.

Drop by tablespoonfuls onto a parchment-lined baking sheet, several inches apart because they spread *a lot*. Bake for 12 minutes, then let cool on a wire rack.

Piña Colada Cookie Bars

Makes an 8x8-inch pan of bars

These tropical treats are a variation of the Coconut Cookie (page 135). This is as close as you'll get to lounging on the beach sipping piña coladas while in the kitchen.

For the topping:
2 ½ cups pineapple tidbits, fresh, frozen, or canned
1 tablespoon cornstarch
½ cup brown sugar
½ teaspoon coconut extract

1 tablespoon soy or coconut milk
For the bars:
½ cup canola oil
¾ cup sugar
¾ cup brown sugar
½ cup coconut milk
¾ teaspoon vanilla extract

1 ½ teaspoons coconut extract
3 cups flour
1 ½ teaspoons baking powder
½ teaspoon salt
1 cup sweetened coconut flakes

For the topping: Combine all ingredients in a small saucepan and stir until mixed. Cook over medium heat for 5–7 minutes or until thickened. Set aside.

For the bars: Preheat oven to 350°F.

In a large bowl, stir together oil, sugar, and brown sugar.

Add the coconut milk, vanilla extract, and coconut extract. Mix until incorporated.

In medium bowl, mix the flour (unsifted), baking powder, and salt. Slowly add to the wet ingredients, until it's completely incorporated.

Stir in coconut flakes.

Put mixture into a parchment-lined 8x8-inch baking pan and bake for 15 minutes. Top with the pineapple mixture, return to the oven, and bake for 7 more minutes. Cool, cut, and eat!

Root Beer Float Cookies

Makes 2
dozen cookies
or 1 dozen
sandwiches

The classic root beer float in cookie form! The cookies on their own are delicately flavored, but the frosting really takes them to the next level. They look really cute if you cut up straws to make mini straws and stick them in the cookies! Or even put root beer barrel candies on top.

Root beer extract is surprisingly easy to find. Craft store baking sections usually carry a variety of extracts, including root beer. It's also readily available on the Internet; it's the same stuff people use to make actual root beer.

½ cup margarine
½ cup sugar
½ cup brown sugar
½ cup soy milk plus 1
   teaspoon vinegar, let sit
   for 5 minutes
½ teaspoon molasses

¼ teaspoon vanilla extract
1 teaspoon concentrated
   root beer extract
½ teaspoon cocoa powder
2 ⅔ cups flour
¾ teaspoon baking soda
¼ teaspoon salt

Frosting:
2 tablespoons margarine
¼ teaspoon concentrated
   root beer extract
2 teaspoons soy milk
1 cup powdered sugar

Preheat oven to 350°F.

Cream together the margarine and sugars.

Add the soy milk/vinegar mixture, molasses, vanilla, root beer extract, and cocoa powder and mix until smooth.

Add the flour, unsifted, baking soda, and salt, and stir until just combined.

Form cookies, a heaping tablespoon each, and slightly flatten on a parchment-lined or greased cookie sheet.

Bake for 8 minutes or until golden, then transfer to a wire rack to cool.

In the meantime, make the frosting. Combine the margarine, root beer extract, and soy milk, and beat until smooth. Gradually add the powdered sugar, adding

more than 1 cup if necessary. Put the frosting in a piping bag or other frosting piping contraption.

When the cookies are cooled, there are two options.

Sandwich cookies: Swirl a generous amount of frosting on top of half the cookies, then place the other halves on top. Pipe a little swirl or star on top of each sandwich cookie, then stick a little straw in each one for decoration.

Regular cookies: Pipe a generous swirl of frosting atop each cookie and stick a straw in the center. You'll probably have leftover frosting, which can be kept in the refrigerator and used with other treats . . . or eaten on its own.

Glazed Rum Raisin Cookies

Makes 18
cookies

Rummy yummy! The quintessential combination of rum and raisins really stands out in this flavorful cookie and is taken to the next level with a lovely rum glaze.

Rummy raisins:
⅓ cup rum
⅔ cup raisins
Dough:
⅓ cup canola oil
¾ cup sugar
3 tablespoons rum, any
    kind

¾ teaspoon vanilla extract
1 ½ teaspoons dark
    molasses
3 tablespoons soy milk
2 cups flour
2 teaspoons baking
    powder

¼ teaspoon salt
Glaze:
3 tablespoons rum,
    reserved from raisins
⅔ cup powdered sugar
1 teaspoon margarine,
    melted

In a small bowl, mix the rum and raisins. Let soak for 20–30 minutes. Meanwhile, preheat the oven to 325°F.

Stir together the oil, sugar, rum, vanilla, molasses, and soy milk in a large bowl.

Sift in the flour, baking powder, and salt. Stir in the rummy raisins, reserving the leftover rum for the glaze.

Drop by large tablespoonfuls onto a lightly greased cookie sheet. Bake for about 12 minutes, or until edges are golden and cookies are firm. Transfer to a wire rack to cool.

In a small bowl, mix the rum (from the raisins; if it measures less than 3 tablespoons, add more), powdered sugar, and melted margarine. If it is too thin, add more powdered sugar.

Glaze each cookie, using a couple teaspoons of glaze to start, then continue until the glaze is all gone.

White Russian Cookies

Makes 18 cookies

These cookies draw you in with an elegant façade, then pack a wild punch like a party in your mouth. It's a culinary mullet without the faux pas.

For the cookies:
⅓ cup canola oil
¾ cup sugar
⅓ cup Kahlúa
3 tablespoons soy milk
2 teaspoons cornstarch
1 teaspoon ground coffee
   beans

2 cups flour
1 teaspoon baking powder
⅛ teaspoon salt
For the icing:
1 tablespoon margarine
1 tablespoon Kahlúa
½ cup powdered sugar

For the chocolate
   shavings:
About 3 ounces dark,
   semisweet, or
   bittersweet chocolate,
   in bar form*

Preheat oven 350°F.

For the cookies: In a large bowl, stir together the oil, sugar, Kahlúa, soy milk, cornstarch, and ground coffee.

Gradually sift in the flour, baking powder, and salt, stirring after each addition.

Form dough into 1 ½-inch balls, then flatten on a lightly greased or parchment-lined cookie sheet.

Bake for 7–8 minutes until golden around the edges and firm in the middle, careful not to burn. Transfer to a wire cooling rack.

For the icing: Melt the margarine in a small bowl, then let cool. Add the Kahlúa, and stir in the powdered sugar until smooth. If it's too liquid, just add a bit more powdered sugar. Set aside.

For the chocolate shavings: First, you're going to need a vegetable peeler (it's not just for carrots and potatoes anymore!). Drag the peeler down the short side of the chocolate bar to make small curls, or "peel" the chocolate against the peeler in the

same way you would zest a lemon for shavings. When finished, immediately freeze the curls because they have a tendency to melt.

Assembly: Drop a dollop of icing atop each cookie, then make rounds again if there's any left over. Make sure the icing is cool, so as not to melt the chocolate. Sprinkle chocolate shavings on each cookie for an elegant touch. Devour! If it's a warm day, you might want to chill these in the fridge to keep the chocolate from melting, but otherwise, an airtight container on the counter is just fine.

*The chocolate is called for in bar form because it's used to make chocolate shavings/curls to sprinkle atop the cookies. If you don't have a bar of chocolate, melt ⅓ cup chocolate chips, pour into a large mass, then chill until hardened. You'll want to do this ahead of time or the chocolate will melt in your fingers when you're shaving it.

Totally Nuts and Seeds!

These recipes showcase a variety of nuts and seeds in simply classic and daringly creative cookies. A whole section is devoted to everyone's favorite legume, the peanut.

PB&J Thumbprints

Makes 16–20 cookies

Sometimes you just want your PB&J in cookie form. I know the feeling. Any kind of jam your heart desires may be used. Raspberry and blueberry are especially delicious.

⅓ cup peanut butter
⅔ cup sugar
2 tablespoons canola oil
1 teaspoon vanilla

⅓ cup soy milk
1 ¼ cups flour
½ teaspoon baking powder
¼ teaspoon baking soda

⅛ teaspoon salt
1 tablespoon peanut butter
About 3 tablespoons fruit-
    flavored jam, any kind

Preheat oven to 350°F.

In a medium-large bowl, stir together the peanut butter, sugar, oil, vanilla, and soy milk. Sift in the flour, baking powder, baking soda, and salt. Stir until combined. Lightly stir in the tablespoon of peanut butter.

Drop by tablespoonfuls onto a parchment-lined or lightly greased cookie sheet. Bake for 5 minutes, then remove from oven. Using your thumb, make an indent in the middle of the cookies. Place about ½ teaspoon jam in each indent.

Bake for an additional 8–11 minutes or until firm.

Soft Peanut Butter Chocolate Chip Cookies

Makes 2 dozen cookies

These cookies are a chocolate peanut butter lover's match made in heaven. Testers all agreed this is some of the best cookie dough they have ever tasted. Leave out the chocolate chips if you're looking for a soft and chewy purely peanut butter cookie.

1 cup peanut butter
2 tablespoons peanut oil
1 cup sugar
1 teaspoon molasses
¾ teaspoon vanilla extract
⅓ cup soy milk

1 ½ cups flour
¾ teaspoon baking soda
¼ teaspoon salt
1 tablespoon peanut butter
Heaping ½ cup chocolate chips

Preheat oven to 350°F.

In a large bowl, stir together the peanut butter, oil, sugar, molasses, vanilla, and soy milk.

Sift in flour, baking soda, and salt. Stir until just combined, then add the chocolate chips. Add a splash of soy milk if the dough is a bit dry or crumbly, or add a touch of extra flour if it's too wet (this can vary based on the kind of peanut butter you use). Lightly stir in the tablespoon of peanut butter.

Roll into balls of heaping tablespoonfuls onto a greased or parchment-lined cookie sheet, flatten, and bake for 9–10 minutes until the edges are firm and the cookies are golden. Let sit on the cookie sheet for a minute, then transfer to a wire rack and let cool.

Peanut Butter Butterscotch Cookies

Makes about 18 cookies

This innovative twist on the classic peanut butter cookie will give your taste buds something to get excited about. Vegan butterscotch extract may be a little hard to find, but it does exist. Check out a gourmet grocery store or the baking aisle of a craft store. A butterscotch chip/ peanut butter fudge version of these is especially delicious.

¼ cup peanut oil
½ cup crunchy peanut
   butter
¼ cup sugar
¾ cup brown sugar
1 tablespoon maple syrup
   or agave nectar

2 tablespoons soy milk
½ teaspoon vanilla extract
½ teaspoon concentrated
   butterscotch extract
1 cup flour
½ teaspoon baking soda
⅛ teaspoon salt

¾ cup total of any or
   a mixture of the
   following: butterscotch
   chips, chopped peanut
   butter fudge (page 51),
   or chopped peanuts

Preheat oven to 350°F.

In a large bowl, stir together the peanut oil, peanut butter, sugars, maple syrup, soy milk, and extracts.

Sift in the flour, baking soda, and salt, then stir in your add-ins.

Form into 1 ½-inch balls and slightly flatten on a parchment-lined cookie sheet. Bake for 10–12 minutes until firm and golden, then transfer to a wire rack to cool.

Peanut Butter Cookie Crumbles

Makes enough crumbles for a piecrust

In addition to using these crumbles for a piecrust, try using them atop ice cream, cakes, or stirred into pudding. Oh, the possibilities!

1 cup peanut butter

¼ cup canola oil

2 teaspoons molasses

1 ½ cups sugar

2 teaspoons vanilla extract

¼ cup soy milk

¼ cup agave nectar or other liquid sweetener

2 tablespoons cornstarch mixed with 2 tablespoons water

2 cups flour

2 teaspoons baking powder

¼ teaspoon salt

Preheat oven to 350°F.

Mix together peanut butter, oil, molasses, sugar, vanilla, soy milk, agave nectar, and cornstarch/water mixture. Stir until smooth. Sift in flour, baking powder, and salt. Mix until combined.

Form dough into cookies and bake on a greased baking sheet for about 12–13 minutes. Crumble on the baking sheet and let sit until cool. If the crumbles are soft after cooling, bake for a few additional minutes until crumbly and crunchy. If crumbling by hand isn't working, pulse in a food processor until crumbly.

Peanut Butter Cups

*Makes about
16 cups using
1-inch molds*

These are just like the packaged peanut butter cups you'll find by the cash register, but vegan and much lovelier. Homemade peanut butter cups may seem like they'd require a tedious process, but they're actually super easy to make! Peanut butter cup molds can be found in the baking section of most craft stores. Mini cupcake liners placed in a mini muffin tin work as well.

Chocolate:
1 ⅓ cups chocolate chips
1 tablespoon shortening

Peanut Butter Filling:
2 teaspoons margarine
¾ teaspoon soy milk
¼ cup light brown sugar, packed

½ cup peanut butter
2 tablespoons graham cracker crumbs
½ teaspoon vanilla extract

Melt the chocolate chips and shortening in your makeshift double boiler (page 6).

Spoon some melted chocolate into the bottoms of the molds, then coat all sides of each cup using your finger and let the chocolate set. Put the rest of the chocolate to the side, keeping it warm, to use for the tops of the peanut butter cups.

Filling: In a small saucepan, melt the margarine over medium-low heat. Add the soy milk and brown sugar and stir until syrupy, about 30 seconds. Stir in the peanut butter, graham cracker crumbs, and vanilla. Continue to stir until the mixture collects into a ball and does not stick to the sides. Remove from heat and transfer the peanut butter filling into a small bowl.

Assembly: Patch up any holes on the chocolate-lined molds with a bit of chocolate. Using 1 generous teaspoon each, place some of the peanut butter filling in each chocolate-coated mold and smooth out the tops.

Using the remainder of the chocolate, coat the tops of the peanut butter cups. Temper the chocolate by letting it set at room temperature, then pop out of the molds and enjoy! Store these in an airtight container, in the refrigerator if it's hot outside.

Peanut Butter Cup Cookies

If you can keep from eating all your peanut butter cups as soon as they're done, go one step further and add chunks of them to wondrously peanut buttery cookie dough. Peanut butter cup cookies are two amazing treats in one sinfully sweet package.

½ cup peanut butter
¼ cup sugar
⅓ cup brown sugar
1 tablespoon peanut or canola oil
¾ teaspoon vanilla extract
⅓ cup soy milk

1 cup flour
¾ teaspoon baking powder
¼ teaspoon salt
8–9 peanut butter cups (page 47),
    coarsely chopped

Preheat oven to 350°F.

In a medium bowl, mix together the peanut butter, sugars, oil, vanilla, and soy milk.

Sift in the flour, baking powder, and salt. Gently incorporate the peanut butter cups into the dough.

Drop by heaping tablespoonfuls onto a greased or parchment-lined cookie sheet. Bake for 10–12 minutes or until firm, let cool on the cookie sheet for a minute, then transfer to a wire rack to cool.

Store in an airtight container.

Peanut Butter Fudge

Makes 16–24 squares, depending on how cut

Peanut butter fudge goes vegan! Fudge can be difficult to make at first because the mixture will crystallize if you don't remove it from the heat at the right moment. Keep trying because peanut butter fudge is worth it! Besides eating it on its own, chopped up pieces are a great addition to Giant Bakery Style Double Chocolate Cookies (page 78) as peanut butter "chips."

¾ cup sugar
⅓ cup soy milk
Dash of salt

1 tablespoon margarine
½ teaspoon vanilla extract
½ cup peanut butter

Place a sheet of parchment paper either in an 8x4-inch loaf pan or similar glass dish. Set aside.

In a medium saucepan over medium-high heat, combine the sugar, soy milk, and salt, stirring frequently until it comes to a boil. Reduce heat to medium, then stir almost constantly until it begins to thicken up, about 10 minutes.

Add the margarine and continue to cook until soft boil stage, or when a drop of the mixture flattens at the bottom and has a toffeelike texture when dropped into a bowl of cold water. Immediately remove from heat and stir in the peanut butter and vanilla.

Transfer the mixture to the prepared pan and spread evenly. Let cool for about 5 minutes at room temperature, then transfer to the fridge until set, about 45 minutes to an hour.

Thin and Crispy Peanut Butter Cookies

Makes about 2 dozen

These classic peanut butter cookies are so light and crispy, they'll melt in your mouth!

½ cup margarine
½ cup peanut butter
½ cup sugar
½ cup brown sugar
2 tablespoons soy milk

1 ¼ cups flour
½ teaspoon baking powder
½ teaspoon baking soda
¼ teaspoon salt

Mix margarine, peanut butter, sugars, and soy milk until smooth.

Combine dry ingredients and add to wet mixture. Beat until well-incorporated.

Roll dough into a log about 2 inches thick. Wrap in plastic wrap and chill for a half hour in the refrigerator.

Preheat oven to 375°F.

Remove dough from refrigerator and slice into ¼-inch rounds. Place on baking sheet lined with parchment paper, about 2 inches apart (they will spread, so it also doesn't matter if there is a flat side from slicing).

Use a fork dipped in sugar to make the crisscross design.

Bake for 7–10 minutes, or until golden brown.

Let sit on baking sheet for an additional minute before transferring to a cooling rack, or they will break apart very easily. Once cooled, however, they are very stable.

Peanut Butter Molasses Cookies

Makes about 25 cookies

These cookies are reminiscent of Mary Jane candies and have an air of sophistication—the more mature cousin of your everyday peanut butter cookie.

1 ½ cups dark brown sugar
½ cup canola oil
⅔ cup peanut butter
¼ cup dark (not blackstrap) molasses
2 ½ cups flour
1 teaspoon baking powder

½ teaspoon baking soda
¼ teaspoon salt
About ¼ cup soy milk
About ½ cup of peanuts, coarsely
  chopped (topping)

Preheat oven to 350°F.

In a large bowl, mix brown sugar, oil, peanut butter, and molasses until well-combined.

In a separate bowl, combine the flour, baking powder, baking soda, and salt. Add the wet ingredients to the dry, and mix until incorporated.

Add the soy milk, a little at a time, and mix until the dough holds together well enough to be formed into balls.

Form the dough into 1-inch balls and press onto a plate of chopped peanuts. Place the disks of dough, peanut side up, on a baking sheet lined with parchment paper.

Bake for 8–10 minutes, or until the edges are firm. Let the cookies sit on the baking sheet for about a minute, then transfer to a wire cooling rack to cool completely.

Peanut Butter Oatmeal Cookies

Makes about 40 cookies

These cookies have a delightfully decadent texture, and the pulverized oatmeal gives them a full-bodied flavor. They're on the small side because when made larger, they're extremely delicate. They'd take longer to bake, too, and I know you don't want to wait around.

½ cup quick-cooking oats
¼ cup margarine
¼ cup shortening
½ cup peanut butter
⅓ cup sugar

½ cup brown sugar
1 tablespoon soy milk
1 teaspoon vanilla
¾ cup flour
1 teaspoon baking soda

½ teaspoon salt
¼ teaspoon cinnamon
  (optional)

Preheat oven to 350°F.

In a food processor, pulse the oats until they're well ground but not quite powdered.

In a large bowl, cream together margarine, shortening, peanut butter, and sugars until smooth. Add soy milk and vanilla, and continue to beat until well-combined.

Sift in the flour, baking soda, salt, and cinnamon (if using). Slowly add the dry mixture to the wet mixture, and beat until combined.

Using a spatula or large spoon, stir in the oats.

Drop by rounded teaspoonfuls onto a parchment-papered cookie sheet. Dip a fork in sugar and make the crosshatches.

Bake for 10–13 minutes, or until the cookies are dark golden brown and feel relatively firm to the touch (you'll know if they're not ready). Let sit on baking sheet for 1 minute, then transfer to a cooling rack.

Peanut Kiss Cookies

Makes about 2 dozen

This classic cookie goes vegan! I found "kiss" chocolate molds at a thrift store and have seen them online as well, but any chocolate mold will work fine with this recipe. I've made chocolates with heart molds and they look very cute!

1 cup chocolate chips
2 teaspoons shortening
"Kiss-" or heart-shaped
   chocolate molds, with
   a capacity of about
   ½ teaspoon melted
   chocolate per mold

⅔ cup peanut butter
⅓ cup maple syrup
½ cup sugar
¼ cup canola oil
1 teaspoon vanilla extract
¼ cup soy milk

2 cups flour
1 teaspoon baking powder
½ teaspoon baking soda
¼ teaspoon salt
3 tablespoons sugar

Melt the chocolate and shortening in a makeshift double boiler or microwave. Fill chocolate molds and let the chocolate temper until hardened, then remove from molds and set aside.

Preheat oven to 350°F.

In a large bowl, stir together the peanut butter, maple syrup, sugar, oil, vanilla, and soy milk. Sift in the flour, baking powder, baking soda, and salt.

Spoon the 3 tablespoons of sugar into a small bowl. Form dough into 1 ½-inch balls, roll each in sugar, and place on a cookie sheet, greased or lined with parchment paper. Do not flatten.

Bake for 11–12 minutes until firm, then remove from oven. Immediately press a chocolate into each cookie. The edges will crack.

Transfer to a cooling rack, then eat!

SECRET LEAVENING AGENTS: CATCH THEM RED-HANDED IF THEY BAIL ON YOU

It totally sucks when cookies fail. Sometimes it's the fault of your leavening agent—baking powder or soda. Use these methods to test if your baking soda and baking powder are fresh and active.

For baking soda: Combine equal amounts of baking soda and vinegar (think elementary school science fair volcanoes). If the baking soda is active, you will see a chemical reaction—bubbling and fizzing! Baking soda is the chemical sodium bicarbonate and needs an acid to react with for the product to rise.

For baking powder: Drop ½ teaspoon into a cup of warm water. If active, it will fizz. Baking powder does not need an acid for a reaction to occur because it contains a chemical that reacts with liquid to create CO_2, making the cookies or other baked goods rise.

Almond Butter Cookies

*Makes about
2 dozen*

One who neglects to venture beyond basic peanut butter into the delicious world of nut butters is very unwise. Think of a nut, any nut, and there's a butter of it. These cookies feature the delectably subtle and sweet almond butter.

½ cup raw, unsalted almond butter
¼ teaspoon almond extract
3 tablespoons canola oil
1 tablespoon agave nectar
⅓ cup sugar
¼ cup brown sugar

¼ cup soy milk
1 ½ cups flour
½ teaspoon baking soda
⅛ teaspoon salt
Slivered or sliced almonds

Preheat oven to 350°F.

In a large bowl, stir together the almond butter, almond extract, oil, agave, sugars, and soy milk. Sift in the flour, baking soda, and salt, and stir until combined.

Drop by heaping tablespoon-sized balls onto a greased cookie sheet and flatten slightly. Sprinkle sliced or slivered almonds on each cookie and press them in with a spatula.

Bake for 8–9 minutes, then transfer to a wire cooling rack.

Almond Cloud Kisses

Makes about 10 sandwiches

These delicate, perfectly round almond cookies are taken to the next level of magnificence when spread with flavorful semisweet chocolate and sandwiched together.

¼ cup canola oil

⅓ cup sugar

2 tablespoons powdered sugar

2 tablespoons soy milk

⅔ cup ground almonds

½ teaspoon almond extract

1 ¼ cups flour

½ teaspoon baking powder

¼ cup chocolate chips

Preheat oven to 350°F.

Beat the oil and sugars in a medium bowl until smooth. Add the soy milk, almonds, and almond extract, and stir until combined.

Sift in the flour and baking powder, and stir until all is incorporated.

Roll dough into tablespoon-sized balls, place on a greased cookie sheet, and flatten ever so slightly. If the dough is too dry and difficult to roll into balls, add a touch of soy milk to the dough.

Bake for 10–11 minutes until the bottoms are golden brown, then transfer to a cooling rack and let cool for 5–7 minutes.

In the meantime, melt the chocolate in a small glass bowl. Turn half the cookies upside down and spoon a little chocolate on their bottoms. Place their other halves on top of them and let sit until the chocolate firms up.

Enjoy!

Cashew Butter Chocolate Chip Cookies

Makes 20 cookies

Fancier than peanut butter cookies, these are filled with rich cashew butter and sweetened with the delicate flavor of agave nectar and a hint of brown sugar.

1 cup cashew butter
3 tablespoons canola oil
½ cup agave nectar
2 tablespoons brown sugar
1 teaspoon vanilla extract
¼ cup soy milk

1 ⅔ cups flour
½ teaspoon baking soda
¼ teaspoon salt
½ cup chocolate chips
⅓ cup chopped cashews (optional)

Preheat oven to 350°F.

In a large bowl, stir together the cashew butter, oil, agave, brown sugar, vanilla, and soy milk until smooth. Sift in the flour, baking soda, and salt, and stir until just combined. Add the chocolate chips and cashews, if using.

Drop by tablespoonfuls onto a parchment-lined cookie sheet, but do not flatten. Bake for 6–8 minutes until golden. Keep an eye on these, because cookies with agave tend to brown quickly.

Let sit on the tray for a couple of minutes, then transfer to a wire cooling rack.

Cashew Chocolate Chip Oatmeal Cookies

Makes about 20 cookies

These cookies are pure bliss. The majority of the fat comes from the amazing, creamy, flavorful cashew butter, so you could call these cookies healthy. No one will ever know, though, because they taste so decadent. Feel free to replace the cashew butter and nuts with a different type of nut for a variation.

⅓ cup creamy roasted cashew butter
1 tablespoon canola oil
¾ cup sugar
⅓ cup soy milk
1 ¼ teaspoons vanilla extract
1 cup flour

½ teaspoon baking soda
¼ teaspoon baking powder
¼ teaspoon salt
1 cup rolled oats
¼ cup chocolate chips
⅓ cup cashew nuts, chopped

Preheat oven to 400° F.

Mix together the cashew butter, oil, sugar, soy milk, and vanilla extract in a medium bowl.

Sift in flour, baking soda, baking powder, and salt. Stir. Add oats, chocolate chips, and cashews, and mix until combined.

Drop by rounded heaping tablespoonfuls onto a cookie sheet, greased or lined with parchment paper, and bake for about 6 minutes until the edges are golden brown. Keep an eye on these, as they'll burn quickly due to the high temperature. Store in an airtight container.

Chewy Caramel Pecan Cookies

Makes 18 cookies

These sweet nutty cookies are loaded with caramel pecans. They are gooey right out of the oven, then firm up to a chewy caramel-y cookie. For a variation, replace the pecans with walnuts.

Caramel Pecans:
⅓ cup margarine
⅔ cup brown sugar
1 tablespoon maple syrup
2 teaspoons soy milk
⅔ cup chopped pecans

Cookies:
¼ cup sugar
¼ cup brown sugar
¼ cup maple syrup
¼ cup canola oil
1 teaspoon vanilla extract

3 tablespoons soy milk
2 cups flour
¾ teaspoon baking soda
⅛ teaspoon salt
16–20 pecan halves

Preheat oven to 350°F.

For the caramel pecans: In a small saucepan, melt the margarine. Stir in the brown sugar, maple syrup, and soy milk. Stir almost constantly over medium heat for about 5 minutes or until bubbly, but still a thick liquid. Add the pecans, then stir until coated for another 15 seconds. It's important that you don't burn the mixture, but it's all right if it's a bit too thick or begins to crystallize. Pour into a small bowl and set aside.

For the cookies: In a large bowl, stir together the sugars, maple syrup, oil, vanilla, and soy milk. Sift in the flour, baking soda, and salt, and mix until combined. Add the caramel pecans. Refrigerate the dough, in the bowl, for 15 minutes. Drop by heaping tablespoonful onto a parchment-lined baking sheet and top each cookie with a pecan half. Do not flatten them. Bake for 7–8 minutes or until spread out and golden. Watch them closely, as they can burn easily. Remove from oven and let sit on the tray for a minute, then lift the parchment out of the tray with the cookies on it and let sit on the surface of your counter to firm up before transferring them to a wire rack, as they will be too delicate right away. Enjoy!

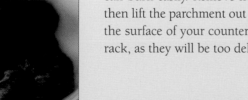

Chinese Almond Cookies

Makes 13–15 cookies

I highly doubt these are authentic, but they are very reminiscent of the cookies I used to get in Chicago's Chinatown after lunch at a Chinese restaurant with my Uncle John. Afterward, we'd go back to his house and he'd give me more cookies, artwork, something he built, odds and ends, and a look in the freezer, where he'd relocate his pet birds after they died. I remember these strange visits quite vividly . . . but I digress. These cookies are delightfully crispy, full of flavor, and one of my favorite recipes in the book.

1 cup slivered almonds
½ cup canola oil
¾ cup sugar
2 teaspoons almond extract

1 ½ cups flour
½ teaspoon baking powder
½ teaspoon baking soda
⅛ teaspoon salt

Preheat oven to 350°F.

Chop the slivered almonds. You still want them to be slivered almonds, not coarsely chopped pieces, but the slivers may be too big right out of the bag.

In a large bowl, mix together the oil, sugar, and almond extract.

Add the flour, baking powder, baking soda, and salt. Gradually stir in the almonds while you incorporate the dry ingredients. Add a splash of soy milk if the dough is crumbly.

Take large portions of dough and flatten on a cookie sheet to make giant palm-sized cookies. Bake for 15–17 minutes until the edges are golden and the centers are very firm. Transfer to a wire rack. They will crisp up as they cool.

Chocolate Nut Florentines

Makes about 10 cookies

These wholesome toffeelike cookies are full of all the nuts, seeds, and dried fruits of your choosing. The chocolate on the edges is the perfect addition. To make a gluten-free version, simply replace the flour with white rice flour or another alternative flour.

⅓ cup sunflower seeds
¼ cup slivered almonds
⅓ cup raisins
¼ cup dried cherries
2 tablespoons flour

¼ cup margarine
¼ cup sugar
1 tablespoon soy milk
¼ teaspoon vanilla extract
½ cup chocolate chips

Preheat oven to 350°F.

In a medium bowl, combine the seeds, nuts, raisins, dried fruit, and flour.

In a saucepan over medium heat, dissolve the sugar in the margarine and cook until thickened like a caramel sauce. Pour this mixture into the nut/seed/fruit mixture and stir until combined. Add the soy milk and vanilla.

Drop the mixture by tablespoonfuls onto a parchment-lined (you will have to pry them off the tray if you don't use parchment) cookie sheet and bake for 7–8 minutes or until firm. Don't burn them.

Remove from the oven and push the edges of the cookies in with a knife to make them look neater and let sit on the tray for 6–8 minutes. Transfer them (still on the parchment) to a plate or two.

Melt the chocolate in the microwave in a zip-top baggie and cut a hole in a bottom corner. Trace the edges of the cookies with chocolate, then let cool at room temperature. When they're completely set, transfer to a wire rack.

Cranberry Almond Cookies

Makes 18 cookies

The classic combination of cranberries and almonds makes for a delicious, subtle cookie. Perfect when you want something modest but satisfying.

½ cup canola oil
½ cup sugar
¼ cup light brown sugar
⅓ cup soy milk plus 2 teaspoons ground
   flaxseed
¾ teaspoon vanilla extract

½ teaspoon almond extract
2 ¼ cups flour
1 teaspoon baking soda
¼ teaspoon salt
⅔ cup slivered almonds
½ cup dried cranberries

Preheat oven to 350°F.

Stir together oil, sugars, soy milk/flaxseed combination, and extracts in a large bowl.

Combine the flour, baking soda, salt, almonds, and cranberries in a medium bowl. Gradually add the dry ingredients into the other bowl, stirring after each addition. Knead to incorporate the cranberries and almonds, if necessary.

Taking golf ball-sized pieces of dough, roll them into balls and flatten on a lightly greased cookie sheet. Bake for 10–12 minutes, let cool on the tray for a minute, then transfer to a wire rack to cool. Store in an airtight container.

Variation: Add ¼ cup dark or semisweet chocolate chips to the batter with the cranberries and almonds.

Sesame Halvah Cookies

Makes 2 dozen cookies

Sesame cookies will take you by surprise with a flavor punch! I sometimes prefer these rich sesame tahini cookies without halvah—try it both ways and see which way you prefer.

3 tablespoons tahini
1 tablespoon canola oil
¾ teaspoon toasted sesame oil
¼ cup soy milk
½ cup sugar
1 teaspoon molasses

1 teaspoon vanilla extract
2 cups flour
1 teaspoon baking soda
½ teaspoon baking powder
½ teaspoon cinnamon
¼ teaspoon ginger
¼ teaspoon salt

¾ cup good quality halvah, chopped (optional)
3 tablespoons sesame seeds
1 tablespoon coarse sugar

Preheat oven to 350°F.

In a large bowl, stir together the tahini, oils, soy milk, sugar, molasses, and vanilla. Sift in the flour, baking powder, baking soda, spices, and salt. Add the halvah, if using, and stir until incorporated.

Stir together the sesame seeds and sugar in a small bowl. Take tablespoon-sized balls of dough and roll them in the sesame and sugar mixture. Place on a lightly greased or parchment-lined cookie sheet and flatten slightly. Repeat with all the dough, then bake for about 12 minutes or until the edges are golden brown and the centers are mostly firm.

Transfer to a wire cooling rack and enjoy!

Sunflower Cookies

Makes 13–15 cookies

These cookies have a wonderfully crispy texture and a crunch thanks to the liberal amount of sunflower seeds. The perfect balance of salty and sweet is bliss for the taste buds. They're extremely delicate, so handle carefully.

⅔ cup canola oil
¾ cup sugar
1 teaspoon vanilla extract
1 tablespoon soy milk
1 ½ cups flour

½ teaspoon baking powder
½ teaspoon baking soda
¼ teaspoon salt
1 cup roasted sunflower seeds

Preheat oven to 350°F.

In a large bowl, mix together the oil, sugar, vanilla, and soy milk.

Add the flour, baking powder, baking soda, and salt. Gradually stir in the sunflower seeds while you incorporate the dry ingredients. Add a splash of soy milk if the dough is crumbly.

Take large portions of dough and flatten on a cookie sheet to make giant palm-sized cookies. Bake for 15–17 minutes until the edges are golden and the centers are very firm. Transfer to a wire rack. They will crisp up as they cool.

Blissfully Chocolate Cookies

This chapter supplies you with the knowledge necessary to indulge in chocolate nirvana, where ignorance is certainly not bliss.

Giant Bakery-Style Double Chocolate Cookies

Makes 8–10 giant cookies (or more small ones)

These cookies will soon rock your world. They are chocolaty, chewy, soft, and decadent, all in a 4-inch diameter. The goal here was to re-create those huge bakery cookies with crispy edges and delicious chewy centers, and the result was far beyond my expectations. Warning: These cookies are highly addictive.

½ cup chocolate chips (for melting)
½ cup soy milk
⅔ cup canola oil
2 teaspoons vanilla

1 ⅓ cups sugar
2 tablespoons cornstarch
2 cups flour
⅔ cup cocoa

2 teaspoons baking powder
¼ teaspoon salt
⅔ cup chocolate chips

Preheat oven to 350°F.

Melt the chocolate chips with ⅓ cup of the soy milk in either a microwave or in a glass dish placed in a saucepan of boiling water (makeshift double boiler).

Pour the melted chocolate and soy milk into a large bowl, then add the rest of the soy milk, oil, vanilla, sugar, and cornstarch.

Add the flour (unsifted), cocoa, baking powder, and salt. Stir until thoroughly mixed, then add the chocolate chips.

Here comes the super fun part! Using your hands (or if you must, a spoon. But live a little! Get your hands covered in the most chocolaty cookie dough ever!), grab handfuls of cookie dough and flatten them out to a little thicker than ½ inch on a cookie sheet lined with parchment paper.

Bake for about 15 minutes (shorter if you made smaller cookies) or until the edges are very firm, and the centers look chewy and feel soft to the touch. Let rest on the cookie sheet for a minute or so, then very carefully transfer to the cooling rack without destroying any cookies. They are completely amazing warm and gooey and still taste divine after cooling off.

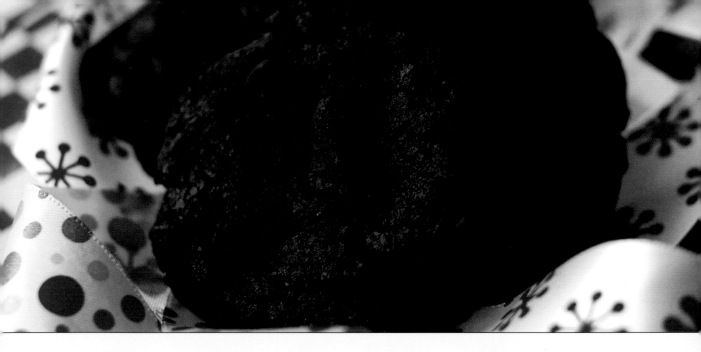

Variations: Replace ¼ teaspoon of the vanilla with almond extract. Replace 1 teaspoon of the vanilla with a fruit extract such as raspberry or strawberry. Add ½ teaspoon cinnamon to the dough. Add 1 teaspoon ground coffee beans or replace 1 teaspoon of the vanilla with coffee extract. Add 2 teaspoons orange zest for chocolate-orange cookies.

DORM ROOM COOKIES: BAKING WITH A TOASTER OVEN

Living without an oven doesn't mean you can't bake cookies! If your dorm rules allow it, invest in a toaster oven and some mini cookie sheets and you can make just about any cookie you could make in a full-size oven. A toaster oven functions as a smaller version of a standard oven.

Toaster ovens heat up pretty quickly, and because all that heat is contained within such a small space, the temperature and baking time may not be the same as if you were using a regular oven. Start by reducing both the temperature and baking time a bit until you figure out how your toaster oven works, then make any adjustments after the first tray is done.

Lemon's Dark Chocolate Truffle Cookies

Makes almost 3 dozen cookies

These intense chocolate cookies melt in your mouth, and the almond extract and orange juice lend a unique magical flavor. Contrary to the name, they don't really have lemons in them. I named them after my friend Lemon, who loves them. She claims to taste a hint of cherry flavor in them, but I'm convinced it's the almond extract.

1 cup flour
⅔ cup cocoa powder
1 teaspoon baking powder
1 cup brown sugar
2 tablespoons canola oil
⅔ cup chocolate chips

1 teaspoon vanilla extract
½ teaspoon almond extract
2 tablespoons orange juice
3 tablespoons soy milk
¼ cup powdered sugar

Preheat oven to 375°F.

Whisk together the flour, cocoa powder, baking powder, and brown sugar in a large bowl, then create a well in the center.

Melt the chocolate chips.

Pour the oil, chocolate chips, vanilla, almond extract, orange juice, and soy milk in the well, then mix the dough until completely combined. If it is crumbly, add a splash or so of soy milk.

Take 2-teaspoon portions of dough, roll them into balls, then roll in powdered sugar and place on a parchment-lined cookie sheet.

Bake for 12–15 minutes, let sit on the tray for a minute, then transfer to a wire cooling rack. Store in an airtight container.

Mini Chocolate Chip Snowball Cookies

Makes 3–4 dozen

These cookies are loaded with mini chips and are very festive-looking when sprinkled with powdered sugar. If you cannot find vegan mini chocolate chips, pulse 2 cups of normal-sized chocolate chips in your food processor until chopped. Alternatively, crushing them in a zip-top bag with a mortar, a hammer, or something else heavy will suffice.

1 ½ cups margarine
¾ cup powdered sugar
1 tablespoon vanilla extract
½ teaspoon salt

3 cups flour
2 cups mini chocolate chips
Additional powdered sugar for sprinkling

Preheat over to 375°F.

In a large bowl, cream the margarine and powdered sugar with an electric mixer until fluffy, then add the vanilla and salt. Gradually sift in the flour.

Stir in the chocolate chips. Form dough into 1 ¼-inch balls and place on ungreased cookie sheets. Bake for 8–9 minutes until firm and golden on the bottom.

Transfer to a wire cooling rack and let cool for 5 minutes.

Using a mesh strainer, sift the powdered sugar atop the cookies until mostly coated. Eat!

Chocolate Chip Cookie Cake

Makes 1 cookie cake

This is your basic chocolate chip cookie cake, a canvas of infinite decorating possibilities! It can be made into any shape you want. I've made the traditional circle shape, a bunny, a paint palette for my high school art show one year, and a peace sign for an annual hippie party I hosted. Basic Buttercream Frosting (page 267) is especially nice on cookie cakes. With some cake decorating tools and piping skills, you can create a really impressive giant cookie.

½ cup margarine
¾ cup sugar
⅓ cup brown sugar
1 ½ teaspoons vanilla extract
¼ cup soy milk

2 ⅓ cups flour
1 teaspoon baking soda
¼ teaspoon salt
⅔ cup chocolate chips

Preheat oven to 350°F.

Cream together the margarine, sugars, and vanilla. Pour in the soy milk, then add the flour, baking soda, salt, and chocolate chips. Stir until just combined.

Form into any shape your heart desires on a parchment-lined cookie sheet. This part is very important, because if you don't make it on parchment it will be difficult to pry from the cookie sheet and it will fall apart.

Bake about 18–20 minutes, depending on shape. Let sit on the tray for 5–10 minutes.

Transfer the cookie cake on the parchment to a wire rack, cool, then decorate!

Pixies

Makes about
3 dozen

These are intensely chocolaty like a chewy iced fudge brownie. They're called "Pixies" because of the powdered sugar. Yum yum yum. The colder the dough is, the more the powdered sugar will adhere to it.

¾ cup cocoa powder
½ cup canola oil
1 ½ cups sugar
2 teaspoons vanilla extract
½ cup soy milk

¼ cup chocolate chips, melted
2 cups flour
2 teaspoons baking powder
¼ teaspoon salt
⅓ cup powdered sugar, more or less

Preheat oven to 350°F.

In a large bowl, mix together the cocoa, oil, sugar, vanilla, and soy milk. Stir in the melted chocolate chips (you know how to melt chocolate, right? Refer to page 6). Add the flour, baking powder, and salt.

Chill the dough, bowl and all, in the freezer for about 10 minutes. The dough should be thick.

Place the powdered sugar in a small bowl. Roll dough into tablespoon-sized balls and then roll in the powdered sugar to coat. Place balls of dough on a cookie sheet lined with parchment paper and flatten.

Bake for about 10–12 minutes, as soon as the edges are firm and the cracks no longer look wet. Remove from oven, sprinkle with leftover powdered sugar, if any is left, and transfer to a wire rack to cool.

Chocolate Jam Thumbprints

Makes 18 cookies

Aww, thumbprint cookies are so cute. But with a fudgy texture and deep chocolate flavor, these are way more fun than your average thumbprint cookie. You can use any kind of jam you like. They're always good with your typical strawberry or raspberry jam, but there are so many possibilities, including peach, blueberry, and apricot!

⅓ cup canola oil
⅔ cup sugar
¼ cup soy milk
¾ teaspoon vanilla extract
¼ teaspoon almond extract

1 ¼ cups flour
½ cup cocoa powder
1 teaspoon baking powder
⅛ teaspoon salt
3–4 tablespoons jam, your choice

Preheat oven to 350°F.

In a medium bowl, mix the oil, sugar, soy milk, and extracts.

Sift in the flour, cocoa, baking powder, and salt, and stir until completely mixed. Add a bit more flour if the dough looks wet.

Shape into tablespoon-sized balls and place on a lightly oiled or parchment-lined baking sheet (do not flatten) and bake for 9 minutes.

Remove from oven and, using your thumb, press into each cookie, making a thumbprint. Put about ½ teaspoon jam on each cookie. Return to the oven and bake for 3 more minutes.

Transfer to a wire rack to cool and enjoy!

Chocolate Marzipan Ravioli

**Makes
18–20 ravioli**

I'm a big fan of using techniques reserved for savory foods when baking (and vice versa). Chocolate marzipan and ravioli shapes are a match made in heaven.

**One batch of Chocolate Sugar Cookie Dough (page 219)
Half a batch of Marzipan (page 268), or store-bought marzipan**

Prepare the chocolate dough and marzipan according to recipes' instructions.

Roll out the chocolate dough and cut into 1 ½-inch strips using a zigzag cutter if you have one. Cut into squares and place a teaspoon-sized ball of marzipan on one of the squares. Top with another square and press around the edges. Repeat with all the dough.

Brush the tops of the raviolis with water if they're cracking.

Place on a parchment-lined baking sheet and bake for about 12 minutes, then let cool on a wire rack.

Orange Chocolate Chunk Cookies

*Makes about
16 cookies*

These cookies are very sophisticated with bakery-style chocolate chunks and a hint of orange flavor. The chocolate-covered orange peel is an optional but wonderful addition. It can be found at specialty stores or you can make it at home.

½ cup canola oil
¾ cup sugar
½ teaspoon vanilla extract
2 teaspoons pure orange extract
⅓ cup soy milk

1 tablespoon maple syrup
2 ½ cups flour
1 teaspoon baking soda
¼ teaspoon salt
¾ cup dark chocolate chunks (about 6 oz.
   of chocolate)

Preheat oven to 375°F.

Combine the oil, sugar, extracts, soy milk, and maple syrup.

Sift in the flour, baking soda, and salt, then stir in the chocolate until evenly incorporated.

Spoon tablespoon-sized portions of dough onto a parchment-lined baking sheet, flatten slightly, and bake for about 10 minutes or until golden on the bottoms and baked all the way through.

Transfer to a wire rack to cool and enjoy!

Variation: Substitute ½ cup of the chocolate chunks with ½ cup chopped chocolate-covered orange peel.

Puppy Chow Cookies

Makes 32 cookies

Like puppy chow? And cookies? Well now they're combined in one confection where chocolate and puppy chow sit atop a caramel-y graham cracker-like cookie. (If for some reason you're wondering why I would make cookies with dog food on top of them, puppy chow is actually a peanut butter and chocolate cereal snack, also referred to as muddy buddies.)

Puppy chow:
⅓ cup peanut butter
3 tablespoons margarine
½ cup chocolate chips
1 ¾ cups rice or oat square cereal
1 ½ cups powdered sugar

Base:
½ cup canola oil
¾ cup brown sugar
3 tablespoons maple syrup
½ teaspoon dark molasses
2 tablespoons applesauce
1 teaspoon vanilla extract

2 ½ cups flour
1 teaspoon baking soda
¼ teaspoon salt
About ½ cup chocolate chips

For the puppy chow: In a microwave-safe bowl, combine the peanut butter, margarine, and chocolate chips and microwave (or do it on the stove, whatever) until everything is just melted. Let cool a bit if it's hot.

Stir in the cereal, and keep stirring until the cereal is completely coated. If it's wet or drippy, chill in the refrigerator for a few minutes, but don't let the chocolate set!

Dump the powdered sugar in a large bowl, then add the chocolaty-peanut-buttery cereal and toss until coated.

Yum, puppy chow. I'm willing to bet there will be some left over after you make the cookies. Lucky you.

For the base: Preheat oven to 350°F.

In a large bowl, stir together the oil, sugar, maple syrup, molasses, applesauce, and vanilla. Add the flour, baking soda, and salt, and stir until combined.

Dump the dough into a zip-top bag (two if it doesn't all fit in one, or do it in two batches if you don't want to waste plastic) and flatten à la the zip-top bag method in Sugar-Crusted Shortbread Cookies (page 236). Chill the bag in the freezer until firm, then cut into squares.

Bake for 12 minutes, then remove from oven.

Immediately place about 4 chocolate chips atop each cookie and let them melt, using a knife to swirl them around.

Top the cookies with about a tablespoon (or however much will stay put, really) of puppy chow. Let the chocolate set and devour!

FREEZER BURN: DON'T LET IT SPOIL YOUR DELECTABLE DESSERTS

While freshly baked cookies are obviously the best, it is acceptable to freeze your cookies or cookie dough. The best way to freeze baked cookies is to lay them out on a parchment-lined cookie sheet and stick the whole cookie sheet in the freezer. When frozen, take the cookie sheet out, wrap the cookies in the parchment, then freeze in a zip-top bag. This method prevents all the cookies from freezing together. When you need individual cookies, take them out of the bag and microwave until warm! It is also possible to freeze cookie dough. The right way is not by sticking your bowl of dough in the freezer, because that will result in a big hunk of bowl-shaped cookie dough. Just like freezing already baked cookies, form your dough into cookies and place on a parchment-lined cookie sheet as if you were baking them, but put the cookie sheet in the freezer until the dough freezes. Then wrap the cookies in the parchment and stick in a zip-top bag. When you want to bake them, lay out the parchment on a cookie sheet, place the cookies evenly on the sheet, then bake as the recipe directs! Your cookies and dough would last for months in your freezer, but they won't taste as fresh if you leave them in there for a long time, so it's best to eat them within a month or two, especially if you're freezing dough, so the leavening agent doesn't lose effect.

No Bakes

No oven needed for these decadent desserts! Perfect for those hot summer days when the last thing you want to do is heat up the house, but you want your cookies.

Chocolate Crispy Cookies

Makes 8–10 cookies

These are more of a confection than a cookie and extremely quick to make, yielding a sweet and crunchy treat.

½ cup chocolate chips
2 tablespoons light corn syrup
2 cups cornflakes
Powdered sugar

Melt the chocolate chips, stir in the corn syrup, then stir in the cornflakes until evenly coated. Form into cookies and put on parchment paper. Sprinkle with powdered sugar and let set.

No-Bake Chocolate Peanut Butter Cookies

Makes about 3 dozen

These are the perfect treat in the hot summer months when you want chocolaty cookies, but would rather not die from the heat of a hot oven. I found the nonvegan version of this recipe in the 1998 Wisconsin Electric Company Cookie Book, then veganized it and tweaked the sweetness level. This little cookie book is a great reference and source of inspiration. Apparently they've been putting out these mini books since the 1940s, when the singular form of cookie was "cooky."

1 ½ cups sugar
½ cup cocoa powder
6 tablespoons margarine
½ cup soy milk

½ cup peanut butter
1 teaspoon vanilla extract
3 cups oatmeal

Bring sugar, cocoa, margarine, and soy milk to a rolling boil in a medium saucepan. Let boil 45 seconds–1 minute, then turn down heat to the lowest setting possible. Add peanut butter, vanilla, and oatmeal. Stir until thick for about 30 seconds. Immediately remove from heat, then drop mixture by spoonfuls onto parchment paper and let cool in the refrigerator or freezer. Store in an airtight container; no need to refrigerate! Enjoy!

*Tip: Any dryness or crumbliness of these cookies is due to boiling/cooking them too long. They can go from the perfect texture to crumbly within seconds, so work fast!

Variations: Replace the peanut butter with a different nut butter, such as almond or cashew. Replace 1 cup of the oats with coarse graham cracker crumbs.

Gooey Butterscotch Cookies

Makes about
25 cookies

Don't worry about boiling the mixture too long. If you undercook it, the cookies may remain obscenely gooey and unmanageable. The spatula is your BFF for this recipe.

⅓ cup soy milk
¼ cup flour
⅓ cup margarine
1 ½ cups brown sugar
¼ teaspoon salt
1 teaspoon vanilla extract
3 cups oats

In a medium saucepan or pot, dissolve the flour into the soy milk. Add margarine and brown sugar, then bring to a boil on medium heat, stirring constantly. Once the mixture reaches a full boil, continue to stir slowly for about 1 minute. Stir in salt and vanilla, then add the oats. Stir the mixture well, until the oats are well-coated, then remove from the heat.

Drop mixture by spoonfuls onto parchment or wax paper, and let cool completely before storing.

No-Bake Cashew Oatmeal Cookies

Makes about 3 dozen

The cousin of baked cashew oatmeal cookies (page 66), the no-bake version is a really gooey sweet treat that is quick and easy to whip up.

½ cup flour
½ cup soy milk
1 ½ cups sugar
6 tablespoons margarine
½ cup cashew butter
1 teaspoon vanilla extract
3 ¼ cups oatmeal

In a medium saucepan, dissolve the flour in the soy milk. Add the sugar and margarine, then bring to a rolling boil at medium-low heat. Let boil 1 minute, stirring frequently. Remove from heat. Add cashew butter, vanilla, and oatmeal. Stir until thick. Drop mixture by spoonfuls onto parchment paper and let cool.

Variations: Add ⅓ cup chopped cashews or chocolate chips when you add the oatmeal. Replace the cashew butter with a different nut butter, such as almond or peanut.

No-Bake Peanut Butter Oatmeal Cookies

Makes about 3 dozen

This is the peanut butter variation of Cashew Oatmeal No Bakes (page 101). Simple, satisfying, and delicious, these will quickly become one of your warm-weather standby treats.

1 ½ cups sugar
½ cup flour
⅓ cup margarine
½ cup soy milk
¾ cup peanut butter, ¼ cup set aside

1 teaspoon vanilla extract
3 cups oats
⅔ cup raisins, chocolate chips, etc.
  (optional)

In a medium saucepan, dissolve the flour in the soy milk. Add the sugar and margarine, then bring to a rolling boil. Let boil 1 minute, then turn down heat to the lowest setting possible. Add ½ cup peanut butter, vanilla, and oats. Stir about 30 seconds, until thick. Remove from heat, then stir in the remaining ¼ cup peanut butter and then the raisins or chocolate chips, if using. Stir lightly until evenly distributed. Drop mixture by spoonfuls onto parchment paper and let cool in the refrigerator or freezer.

DIY Versions of Mass-Produced Cookies

Going vegan often means giving up some of the packaged junk foods you once loved. But now you can take matters into your own hands and re-create these favorites in your kitchen! You can make your own purely decadent treats untouched by preservatives and hidden animal ingredients.

Double Peanut Butter Sandwich Cookies

Makes about 10 sandwich cookies

Just like the popular peanutty sandwich cookies, these are loaded with maximum peanut butter flavor and wholesome goodness! Perfecting this recipe was a long, epic battle of arduous experimentation, but with the results to show for it.

If you don't have or don't want to buy oat flour, you can simply pulverize oats in your food processor.

¼ cup margarine, melted
⅓ cup creamy peanut
   butter
⅔ cup sugar
½ teaspoon vanilla extract
1 tablespoon soy milk

⅔ cup flour
2 tablespoons ground oats
   (oat flour)
⅛ teaspoon salt
1 tablespoon creamy
   peanut butter

Cream filling:
2 tablespoons shortening
¼ cup creamy peanut
   butter
⅔ cup powdered sugar
¼ teaspoon vanilla extract

Preheat oven to 350°F.

In a large bowl, mix the margarine, peanut butter, sugar, vanilla, and soy milk. Gradually stir in the flour, then add the ground oats and salt. Start mixing with your hands here. Add the tablespoon of peanut butter. If the dough isn't holding together, add a tiny splash of soy milk to help.

Taking portions of dough, about 1 ½ teaspoons each, form peanut-shaped cookies a little less than ¼-inch thick. Place on a parchment-lined cookie sheet (it's best to use parchment for these because a greased cookie sheet will make the cookies too oily). Bake for 10–12 minutes until firm and golden. Don't burn them, but be sure to bake long enough or they won't harden up to a nice crispy, crunchy texture. Remove from oven and let sit on the cookie tray for at least 5 minutes, so they don't break, before transferring to a cooling rack.

While the cookies are cooling, make the cream filling. Stir together the shortening and peanut butter until completely mixed. Gradually add the powdered sugar and vanilla. Stir until completely mixed. Don't add any soy milk to the mixture, or the cookies will become soggy. If it's too powdery and not holding together, add more peanut butter.

To assemble the cookies, place about 2 teaspoons peanut butter cream filling on half the cookies, then place the other halves atop them and very carefully squeeze together. Eat!

Graham Crackers

Makes about 10 graham crackers or 3 cups crumbs

These homemade grahams are versatile, all-purpose, and downright delicious! Dip in soy milk, spread with peanut butter, use for s'mores, or eat on their own! Throw in your food processor to make graham cracker crumbs to use for piecrusts or in recipes such as Peanut Butter Cups (page 47). Store crumbs in the freezer in an airtight container for convenience. If you'd like to double the recipe, make two separate batches unless you have a food processor with a very large capacity.

¾ cup all-purpose flour

1 cup whole wheat pastry or white whole wheat flour

½ cup rye flour

½ cup sugar

1 teaspoon baking powder

½ teaspoon baking soda

½ teaspoon cinnamon

⅛ teaspoon salt

¼ cup margarine

3 tablespoons agave nectar or maple syrup

2 tablespoons dark molasses

¼ cup soy milk, 1 tablespoon reserved

1 teaspoon vanilla extract

Optional:

1 tablespoon sugar

½ teaspoon cinnamon

In a large food processor, combine the flours, sugar, baking powder, baking soda, cinnamon, and salt. No need to sift.

Pulse until relatively uniform. Add the margarine, about a tablespoon at a time, and continue to process until the mix looks like small pebbles are scattered throughout.

Add the agave or maple syrup, molasses, 3 tablespoons of soy milk, and vanilla. Process on medium until the dough collects into a ball, adding the remaining tablespoon of soy milk if the dough is too dry, plus more, if necessary.

Wrap the dough in plastic wrap and chill in the freezer for 25 minutes or in the fridge for a couple hours.

Preheat oven to 350°F.

Using a floured rolling pin, roll out the dough about ¼-inch thick on a floured surface, half of it at a time, if necessary. Using a knife, cut dough into 2x4-inch rectangles or use cookie cutters for shapes. Place on a cookie sheet lined with parchment paper, or greased. With the knife, lightly score the grahams down the middle, widthwise, but don't cut all the way through. Poke them on both sides with a fork to get that classic graham cracker look. If using, mix together the cinnamon and sugar in a small bowl, then sprinkle atop the grahams.

Bake for about 15–18 minutes until the edges are hard, but not burned. The grahams won't be crunchy directly out of the oven, but will firm up when cool. Store in an airtight container, away from any other baked goods, as the crackers will absorb moisture and lose crunchiness.

Chocolate Graham Crackers

Makes about 8 large graham crackers or 3 cups crumbs

These are the homemade version of classic chocolate grahams. They taste great on their own, but are amazing paired with nut butter, frosting, or a glass of soy milk! Like the regular grahams, they can be thrown in your food processor to make chocolate graham cracker crumbs to use for piecrusts or stored in the freezer in an airtight container for convenience. If you'd like to double this recipe, make two separate batches.

¾ cup all-purpose flour
¾ cup whole wheat pastry
   or white whole wheat
   flour
¼ cup rye flour
½ cup cocoa powder

⅔ cup sugar
1 teaspoon baking powder
½ teaspoon baking soda
½ teaspoon cinnamon
⅛ teaspoon salt
3 tablespoons canola oil

3 tablespoons agave nectar
   or maple syrup
2 teaspoons dark molasses
¼ cup soy milk, 1
   tablespoon reserved
1 ½ teaspoons vanilla
   extract

In a large food processor, combine all the dry ingredients. No need to sift.

Pulse until relatively uniform. Add the oil, about a tablespoon at a time, and continue to process until the mix looks like small pebbles are scattered throughout.

Add the agave or maple syrup, molasses, 3 tablespoons of soy milk, and vanilla. Process on medium until the dough collects into a ball, adding the remaining tablespoon of soy milk if the dough is too dry, plus more, if necessary.

Wrap the dough in plastic wrap and chill in the freezer for 25 minutes or in the fridge for a couple hours.

Preheat oven to 350°F.

Using a floured rolling pin, roll out the dough about ¼-inch thick on a floured surface, half of it at a time, if necessary. Use a knife to cut dough into 2x4-inch rectangles or use cookie cutters for shapes. Place on a cookie sheet lined with parchment paper, or greased. With the knife, lightly score the grahams down the middle, widthwise, but don't cut all the way through. Poke them on both sides with a fork to get that classic graham cracker look.

Bake for about 15–18 minutes until the edges are hard, but not burned. The grahams won't be crunchy directly out of the oven, but will firm up when cool. Store in an airtight container, away from any other baked goods, as the crackers will absorb moisture and lose crunchiness.

Peanut Butter Graham Crackers

Makes about 10 graham crackers or 3 cups crumbs

You've probably had peanut butter spread on regular graham crackers, but how about baked into them? Didn't think so! It's time to experience this treat!

¾ cup all-purpose flour
1 cup whole wheat pastry
 or white whole wheat
 flour
½ cup rye flour
⅔ cup brown sugar
1 teaspoon baking powder

½ teaspoon baking soda
½ teaspoon cinnamon
⅛ teaspoon salt
1 tablespoon peanut oil
⅓ cup peanut butter
3 tablespoons agave nectar
 or maple syrup

1 ½ tablespoons dark
 molasses
¼ cup soy milk, plus more
 if necessary
1 teaspoon vanilla extract

In a large food processor, combine the flours, brown sugar, baking powder, baking soda, cinnamon, and salt. No need to sift.

Pulse until relatively uniform. Add the oil and peanut butter, about a tablespoon at a time, and continue to process until the mix looks like small pebbles are scattered throughout. Add the agave or maple syrup, molasses, soy milk, and vanilla. Process on medium until the dough collects into a ball, adding the remaining tablespoon of soy milk if the dough is too dry, plus more, if necessary. Wrap the dough in plastic wrap and chill in the freezer for 25 minutes or in the fridge for a couple hours.

Preheat oven to 350°F.

Using a floured rolling pin, roll out the dough about ¼-inch thick on a floured surface, half of it at a time, if necessary. Use a knife to cut dough into 2x4-inch rectangles or use cookie cutters for shapes. Place on a cookie sheet lined with parchment paper, or greased. With the knife, lightly score the grahams down the middle, widthwise, but don't cut all the way through. Poke them on both sides with a fork to get that classic graham cracker look.

Bake for about 14–15 minutes until the edges are hard, but not burned. The grahams won't be crunchy directly out of the oven, but will firm up when cool. Store in an airtight container, away from any other baked goods, as the crackers will absorb moisture and lose crunchiness.

MARGARINE VERSUS OIL: IT'S A DRAW

Both margarine and oil play the same role in baking—they add the fat that creates the decadent texture essential to a good cookie. However, the end result of some recipes that use margarine may not be the same if you substitute oil, and vice versa.

Margarine is best for creating the crispy, melt-in-your-mouth textures found in shortbread or chocolate chip cookies. It holds sugar cookie dough together well because beating the margarine with sugar creates an emulsion perfect for thick doughs. Although vegan-friendly margarine is easy to find nowadays, it can be tough on the budget, especially when used in the quantities baked goods call for.

Oil creates chewy, soft cookies. It's much cheaper than margarine and easier to work with, but for certain cookies oil won't yield the right texture. I try to use oil in my recipes as much as possible, but sometimes margarine makes enough of a difference that it's worth the extra effort and expense. Still, if you want to experiment with replacing margarine with oil in a recipe, substitute the margarine with ⅔ the amount of oil and decrease the soy milk or other liquid in the recipe. For example, if a recipe calls for 1 cup of margarine and ¼ cup soy milk, use ⅔ cup oil and leave out the soy milk. If necessary, you can add more soy milk later to get the right consistency.

Oatmeal Cream Pies

Makes 9 cookie pies

No one will be a Debbie Downer anymore with this classy, grown-up version of the similar store-bought sweets.

⅔ cup canola oil
¾ cup brown sugar
½ cup sugar
2 teaspoons molasses
1 teaspoon vanilla extract
¼ cup soy milk
1 ¾ cups flour

1 ½ cups quick oats
1 teaspoon baking soda
⅛ teaspoon cinnamon
½ teaspoon salt
Cream:
Vegan marshmallow cream
　OR

2 tablespoons vegetable
　shortening
2 tablespoons margarine
1 cup powdered sugar
½ teaspoon vanilla extract
1 tablespoon soy milk

Preheat oven to 350°F.

In a medium-large bowl, mix together the oil, sugars, molasses, vanilla, and soy milk.

Add the flour, oats, baking soda, cinnamon, and salt. Add an extra splash of soy milk if the dough is dry.

Take golf ball-sized portions of dough and place on a lightly greased or parchment-lined baking sheet. Flatten ever so slightly and bake for 7 minutes.

In the meantime, make the filling (if using in place of marshmallow cream). Whisk together the shortening and margarine with a fork. Add the powdered sugar gradually, mixing after each addition, and alternate adding the vanilla and soy milk.

Let the cookies cool. Spread a spoonful of marshmallow cream or frosting on the inside of one half and top with the other half.

Soy Milk's Favorite Cookies

Makes 3–4 dozen

I'd been meaning to come up with a recipe for this classic cookie for a long time. The opportunity finally presented itself shortly after I'd had my wisdom teeth removed and I really wanted cookies 'n' cream frosting. There were no cookies in the house, and I was in no state to drive anywhere to buy them. This was the perfect time to create my very own chocolate wafer-like cookies that would sandwich together, encasing a sweet vanilla cream.

Besides eating these cookies on their own, they are great for making cookies 'n' cream frosting, milkshakes, ice cream, cupcakes, and so much more. For the sake of not having to clean your beaters between making the cookies and the filling, we're going to make the cream filling first. Or, if you're using a fork to make it, do it in whatever order you want. The shortening is essential in the cream filling for a stiff, nonrunny texture, so no substitutions!

Cream filling:

¾ cup vegetable
shortening

¾ teaspoon vanilla extract

3 cups powdered sugar,
sifted

Cookies:

½ cup vegetable
shortening

⅓ cup margarine

1 cup sugar

3 tablespoons maple syrup
or other liquid sugar

¼ cup soy milk, plus more
as needed

1 ½ teaspoons vanilla
extract

2 ⅓ cups flour

½ teaspoon baking soda

¾ cup cocoa powder

¼ teaspoon salt

For the cream filling: In a medium-large bowl, mix the shortening, vanilla, and a small portion of the powdered sugar with either an electric mixer or a fork. Gradually add more powdered sugar. You may not need all of it, because too much will make it dry and crumbly. Do not add soy milk to the cream filling, as the assembled cookies may lose their crispiness or get soggy. If it seems a bit too dry, place atop the warm oven or microwave for 10 seconds. Set aside, but not in the fridge because it will turn into a solid mass of cream filling.

For the cookies:

Preheat oven to 325°F.

In a large bowl, cream the shortening, margarine, and sugar together until smooth. Add maple syrup, soy milk, and vanilla. Blend until all ingredients are combined and there is no crumbliness.

Sift in flour, baking soda, cocoa, and salt in parts, and beat after each addition. If the dough is too dry, add a little soy milk. The dough should be slightly stiff, and you should be able to knead it. If it's too sticky, add some more flour.

Roll the dough into a log, freeze for about 15 minutes, then slice into ⅛-inch-thick rounds. Place cookies on a parchment-lined baking sheet.

Once your cookies are all cut out, bake for 8–10 minutes, watching very, very carefully. They can go from perfectly done to burned in 30 seconds. They are done when the edges and center are firm, but not hard. Remove from the oven and transfer cookies to a wire cooling rack with a spatula. They harden as they cool.

Assembly: Using about 1 teaspoon frosting for each sandwich cookie, put the frosting onto one half, top with another cookie, and press together very carefully as the cookies are delicate. Repeat with all cookies and enjoy doing whatever you like to do with these cookies!

VARIATIONS:

Chocolate Cream: Replace ½ cup powdered sugar with cocoa powder.

Strawberry Cream: Replace ¾ teaspoon vanilla in the cream filling with 1 teaspoon strawberry extract.

Peppermint: Reduce vanilla in the cookie dough to ½ teaspoon and add 1 teaspoon peppermint extract. For the cream filling, reduce vanilla to ¼ teaspoon and add ¾ teaspoon peppermint extract and 5–6 finely smashed candy canes.

Peanut Butter Cream: In the cream filling, reduce the shortening to ½ cup and add ¼ cup peanut butter and a dash of salt.

Halloween Cookies: Add orange (or a mix of red and yellow) food coloring to the cream filling. If desired, replace ½ teaspoon vanilla with orange extract.

Cookies 'n' Cream: Overkill? Nay. Add 12–14 smashed chocolate cookies to the cream filling.

Mocha Cream: Replace the soy milk in the cookie dough with cool coffee. Add 1 tablespoon ground coffee beans to the cookie dough and 2 teaspoons ground coffee beans to the cream filling.

New colors and flavors: Replace the vanilla in the cream filling with any flavor extract you desire. Add food coloring for a colorful treat.

Dip the cookies in chocolate!

Cookies 'n' Cream Cookies

**Makes about
18 cookies**

America's favorite cookie, in a cookie! The vegan version will rock your world more than a packaged, preservative-laden version ever could!

⅓ cup canola oil
¾ cup sugar
¼ cup maple syrup
2 tablespoons applesauce
2 tablespoons soy milk
1 teaspoon vanilla extract

2 ½ cups flour
1 teaspoon baking soda
¼ teaspoon salt
¼ cup chocolate chips
8–9 Oreo-style cookies (page 112 or store bought), chopped coarsely, about 1 ¾ cups

Preheat oven to 350°F.

Stir together the oil, sugar, maple syrup, applesauce, soy milk, and vanilla. Sift in the flour, baking soda, and salt, and stir until combined.

Add the chocolate chips and cookies.

Drop 2-tablespoon portions of dough onto a parchment-lined cookie sheet and bake for 10–12 minutes or until firm and golden.

Transfer to a wire cooling rack.

Rice Crispy Treats

Makes an 8x8-inch tray of squares

You can make vegan rice crispy treats that taste just like the original kind with common ingredients found in any grocery store. The sticky sweetness of corn syrup (I never said they were health food) paired with vanilla duplicate the flavor and gooeyness of marshmallow in these treats. Oh, and they're ridiculously easy to make.

⅔ cup light corn syrup
½ cup sugar
2 tablespoons margarine
¾ teaspoon vanilla
3 ¼ cups crispy rice cereal

Pour the cereal into a large glass bowl and line an 8x8-inch pan with wax paper. Set aside.

Heat the corn syrup in a small saucepan over medium heat, then add the sugar.

Stirring frequently, bring to a boil, then add the margarine. Stir until melted, then add the vanilla and incorporate.

Pour the mixture over the cereal. Stir with a spatula until completely coated, then press the mixture into the pan. Let set, then cut into squares. That's it!

Before the treats set, the mixture will be pretty gooey and will not hold together well, but after a few hours they'll be perfect.

Delightful Coconut Caramel Butter Cookies

Makes about
36 cookies

You may want to make the cookie part the day before the caramel and chocolate because the number of steps in this recipe makes it a little tedious—but worth it in the end, especially if you score some leftover coconut caramel!

For the cookies:
¾ cup margarine
½ cup sugar
½ teaspoon vanilla extract

2 cups flour
½ teaspoon baking powder
¼ teaspoon salt
2–3 teaspoons soy milk, if necessary

Preheat oven to 350°F.

Cream together the margarine, sugar, and vanilla until smooth. Sift in the flour, baking powder, and salt and stir until just combined. Add the soy milk if the dough is dry or won't hold together.

Roll the dough out ¼-inch thick and cut out cookies with a 1 ½-inch circular cookie cutter. If you don't have a 1 ½-inch cookie cutter, many lids of spice containers are around this size, so save your old spice container lids for cookie purposes! Then, using a knife or a teeny, tiny, circular cookie cutter if you have one, cut little holes in the centers of the cookies.

Place on a parchment-lined baking sheet (don't toss the parchment after baking—we'll use it twice more in this recipe) and bake for 10–11 minutes, until lightly golden. Transfer to a wire rack to cool.

For the coconut caramel:
1 ¾ cups sweetened flaked
    coconut
⅓ cup margarine
¾ cup brown sugar
⅓ cup soy milk
⅓ cup agave nectar
⅛ teaspoon salt
½ teaspoon vanilla extract

Toast the coconut at 400°F on the parchment-lined baking sheet for 12 minutes, or until lightly golden. Set aside.

In a medium saucepan, combine the margarine, brown sugar, soy milk, agave, and salt. Cook over medium heat, stirring frequently, until a small spoonful of the syrup dropped in a bowl of cold water holds its shape (soft boil stage), about 15 minutes. Cook for an additional 2 minutes after this point, then remove from heat and add the vanilla and coconut. Transfer the coconut caramel to a small bowl and chill until it's a thick, spreadable consistency.

Assembly:

1 ¼ cups chocolate chips   1 teaspoon shortening

Neatly spread each cookie with coconut caramel and place on the parchment-lined baking sheet. Don't skimp on the caramel, but don't use so much that it's falling over the edges. Pop the cookie tray in the freezer for about 5 minutes to let the caramel set.

Meanwhile, melt the chocolate and shortening in a wide, shallow glass dish in your makeshift double boiler/pan of boiling water. Dip the bottom of each cookie in the chocolate, removing the excess chocolate on the side of the dish, then place the cookie back on the parchment. Repeat for all cookies.

Transfer the remaining chocolate to a zip-top bag, cut the corner off to make a small hole, then drizzle chocolate on each cookie.

Let the chocolate set at room temperature, and then you're done. Finally!

VARIATIONS:

Fudge Stripes: Omit the coconut caramel and you've made fudge stripe cookies!

Saler-NO Butter Cookies: Instead of cutting out the cookies with a circular cookie cutter, opt for a flower-shaped one. Omit the coconut caramel and chocolate. Stick on fingers and proceed to eat.

Chocolate Peppermint Wafer Cookies

Makes about 2 dozen

These peppermint chocolate cookies are just as satisfying as the Girl Scout version! Pure peppermint extract is a world apart from imitation, so substituting any kind of artificial flavor for the real thing is simply not worth it, especially for these addictive cookies.

½ cup margarine
¾ cup sugar
1 ¾ teaspoons peppermint extract
½ teaspoon vanilla extract

2 tablespoons soy milk
3 tablespoons chocolate chips, melted
1 ¼ cups flour
⅔ cup cocoa powder

½ teaspoon baking soda
2 cups chocolate chips
1 tablespoon shortening

Cream together the margarine, sugar, and extracts. Add the soy milk and melted chocolate. Continue to mix until smooth.

Sift in the flour, cocoa powder, and baking soda, gradually adding extra splashes of soy milk if necessary to hold the dough together.

Roll the dough into a log about 1 ½-inch wide and wrap in either plastic or parchment paper. Freeze for at least 30 minutes.

Preheat oven to 350°F.

Slice rounds of dough ⅛- to ¼-inch thick and flatten with your palm onto a parchment-lined cookie sheet (if you wrapped the dough in parchment, you can use that). If the dough is cracking or too hard, let it sit out for 5–10 minutes, and it will begin to soften.

Bake cookies for about 12 minutes, until firm. They will harden up a bit once they cool, but not a lot, so make sure they aren't too soft when you remove them from the oven. Let cool on a wire rack.

In the meantime, melt your chocolate and shortening in a glass bowl in a pan of boiling water over the stove.

Dip cookies into the chocolate, remove with a fork, and place on a parchment-lined cookie sheet.

Let sit at room temperature until the chocolate is hardened, then eat! These are really good cold from the refrigerator, but they don't need to be refrigerated unless it's a really hot day.

Vanilla Wafer Cookies

*Makes 20–24
cookies*

These cookies taste great with a glass of cold almond milk! They aren't exactly like their store-bought counterpart, but they hold their own. Actually, they're pretty scrumptious.

⅓ cup margarine
⅓ cup sugar
⅓ cup brown sugar

2 teaspoons vanilla extract
1 cup flour
½ teaspoon baking powder
¼ teaspoon salt

Soy milk to hold the dough together

Preheat oven to 325°F.

Cream together the margarine, sugars, and vanilla extract in a medium bowl.

Add the flour, baking powder, salt, and soy milk (if the dough is crumbly or won't hold together).

Take 2-teaspoon portions of dough, roll into balls, then flatten on a parchment-lined baking sheet.

Bake for 18–22 minutes or until firm. They will crisp up as they cool.

Fruity Cookies

When life gives you lemons, make cookies! These recipes showcase all kinds of fruit at their finest—in cookies.

Autumn Clouds
Pumpkin Chocolate Chip Cookies

*Makes
1–2 dozen,
depending on
size*

These fluffy, melt-in-your-mouth pumpkin cookies were the result of a quest to make chewy pumpkin cookies. While the result wasn't exactly what I planned, these were too good to forget about. You don't have to wait to make them in the fall, because pumpkin chocolate chip cookies are wonderful any time of the year!

1 cup pumpkin puree
⅔ cup sugar
1 teaspoon molasses
¼ cup maple syrup
⅔ cup canola oil
2 cups flour
1 teaspoon baking powder

1 teaspoon cinnamon
¾ teaspoon ginger
¼ teaspoon allspice
⅛ teaspoon salt
½ cup chocolate chips (you could replace these with raisins, nuts, or other dried fruit)

Preheat oven to 350°F.

In a large bowl, mix together the pumpkin, sugar, molasses, maple syrup, and oil. Sift together the flour, baking powder, spices, and salt and add to the wet ingredients. Stir in the chocolate chips.

Drop by huge (scone-sized) or normal-sized spoonfuls onto a cookie sheet lined with parchment paper. Bake for about 12–14 minutes until firm, depending on size. Transfer to a cooling rack and enjoy! These taste amazing warm out of the oven, but the flavors are really enhanced overnight or even just a few hours after baking.

Apricot Almond Cookies

Makes about 20 cookies

I was on an apricot kick when I made this recipe. Basically, I threw apricots and a bunch of other favorite ingredients in a bowl and the dough for these dainty treats was born. They have a delicate, sophisticated flavor from the apricot jam and are perfect with a cup of tea.

¼ cup canola oil
¼ cup maple syrup or
   agave nectar
3 tablespoons sugar
¾ teaspoon almond
   extract

½ teaspoon vanilla extract
¼ cup apricot jam
2 tablespoons soy milk
1 ½ cups flour
½ teaspoon baking soda
⅛ teaspoon salt
½ cup chopped almonds

⅓ cup chopped dried
   apricots
Topping:
3 tablespoons apricot jam
2 teaspoons water
Whole almonds

Preheat oven to 350°F.

In a large bowl, stir together the oil, maple syrup, sugar, extracts, jam, and soy milk.

Sift in the flour, baking soda, and salt. Stir until nearly combined, then add the almonds and dried apricots.

Drop the dough by tablespoonfuls onto a lightly greased cookie sheet and bake for about 12 minutes.

In the meantime, stir together the topping ingredients in a small bowl, except for the almonds.

Transfer the cookies to a wire rack after cooling on the cookie sheet for about a minute.

Drop about ½ teaspoon of topping on each cookie, then press a whole almond in the center.

Chewy Banana-Banana Cookies

Makes about 2 dozen

All the banana cookie recipes I've come across aren't just banana; they're usually banana oatmeal, banana nut, banana-whatever. But this recipe showcases just the banana, in all its glory, unhindered by another main ingredient trying to steal its spotlight. Call these banana-banana cookies, if you will. They're effortless to make, too.

Banana (and other ingredients that contain a lot of moisture, such as pumpkin or applesauce) cookies have a tendency to come out fluffy, so any more than ⅓ cup mashed banana may result in a puffy cookie rather than a chewy one. It's also important to flatten them on the baking sheet until they are thin.

⅓ cup mashed, very ripe banana (about 1 small banana)
⅓ cup canola oil
½ cup sugar
⅓ cup brown sugar

1 teaspoon vanilla extract
½ teaspoon dark or blackstrap molasses
1 teaspoon ground flaxseed

3 tablespoons powdered sugar
1 ½ cups flour
½ teaspoon baking soda
¼ teaspoon salt
¼ teaspoon cinnamon

Preheat oven to 350°F.

In a large bowl stir together the mashed banana, oil, sugars, vanilla, molasses, flaxseed, and powdered sugar.

Pour in the flour (don't sift), then add the baking soda, salt, and cinnamon.

Taking 2-teaspoon portions of dough, flatten them ⅛- to ¼-inch thick on a greased cookie sheet. The dough probably will be a bit sticky, but that's normal. It helps to wet your hands a little bit or wash your hands every so often when flattening. You'll probably need to bake these in two batches. Bake for 8–9 minutes until the centers are very firm and the edges almost hard. Let sit on the tray for a couple

minutes before transferring to a wire rack. They may be a little bit difficult to get off the tray, but that's normal and means they'll be wonderfully chewy.

Variation: If you must, add ⅓ cup chopped walnuts or chocolate chips (smashed in a baggie with a hammer) to the dough.

Chewy Pumpkin Spice Cookies

*Makes about
2 dozen*

Finally, chewy pumpkin cookies! Pumpkin cookies, like banana cookies, are inclined to come out fluffy, so any more than ⅓ cup pumpkin will probably make them less chewy. Don't worry, the flavor will be uncompromised. It's also important to flatten them thinly on the baking sheet.

⅓ cup canned pumpkin (not pumpkin pie
    mix)
⅓ cup canola oil
½ cup sugar
⅓ cup brown sugar
1 teaspoon vanilla extract
½ teaspoon dark or blackstrap molasses
1 teaspoon ground flaxseed
3 tablespoons powdered sugar

1 ½ cups flour
½ teaspoon baking soda
¼ teaspoon salt
1 ¼ teaspoons cinnamon
½ teaspoon ground ginger
⅛ teaspoon cloves
¼ teaspoon allspice
⅛ teaspoon nutmeg

Preheat oven to 350°F.

In a large bowl stir together the pumpkin, oil, sugars, vanilla, molasses, flaxseed, and powdered sugar.

Pour in the flour (don't sift), then add the baking soda, salt, and spices. If the dough is too sticky, add a bit more flour.

Taking 2-teaspoon portions of dough, flatten them to about ⅛ inch on a greased cookie sheet. You'll probably need to bake these in two batches. Bake for 9–10 minutes until the centers are very firm and the edges almost hard. Let sit on the tray for a couple minutes before transferring to a wire rack. They may be a bit difficult to get off the tray, but that's normal and means they'll be soft and chewy.

Optional: Add ⅓ cup chocolate chips to the batter.

Coconut Cookies

Makes about 25 cookies

These cookies are fairly sweet, and have a chewy, slightly crispy texture. The coconut flakes on top get lightly toasted, adding a touch of elegance.

½ cup margarine or coconut oil
½ cup sugar
½ cup brown sugar
⅓ cup coconut milk
½ teaspoon vanilla extract

1 teaspoon coconut extract
2 cups flour
1 teaspoon baking powder
¼ teaspoon salt
1 cup sweetened coconut flakes, plus
    some for garnish

Preheat oven to 350°F.

In a large bowl, beat the margarine, sugar, and brown sugar with an electric mixer.

Add the coconut milk, vanilla extract, and coconut extract. Mix until incorporated.

In medium bowl, mix the flour (unsifted), baking powder, and salt. Slowly add to the wet ingredients until they're fully mixed in, then stir in coconut flakes.

Form into 1 ½-inch balls. Place on a cookie sheet, either lightly greased or lined with parchment paper. Flatten slightly, leaving about 1 ½ inches between each one. Sprinkle a small amount of coconut flakes onto the top of each, and lightly pat down.

Bake for 10–13 minutes or until the edges are golden brown and the cookies are still a bit soft. Let sit on cookie sheets for about a minute, then transfer to a wire cooling rack.

Glazed Lime Cookies

These cookies have a light citrus taste, emphasized by the flavorful glaze. Think warm summer day with a glass of lemonade and some glazed lime cookies.

¾ cup margarine

¼ cup canola oil

1 cup powdered sugar

1 tablespoon lime zest
  (3–4 limes)

2 tablespoons lime juice
  (2–3 limes)

2 teaspoons lemon zest
  (1–2 lemons)

2 teaspoons vanilla extract

2 ¼ cups flour

¼ teaspoon baking soda

¼ teaspoon baking powder

¼ teaspoon salt

For the glaze:

1 cup powdered sugar

1 teaspoon lime zest

1 tablespoon lime juice

1 teaspoon light corn
  syrup

About 2 teaspoons water

Preheat oven to 350° F.

In a large bowl, beat together margarine and canola oil until fluffy. Add the powdered sugar, and bring the mixture back to a fluffy consistency. Add the lime zest, lime juice, lemon zest, and vanilla extract, and beat until even once again, about 1 minute.

Add the flour, baking soda, baking powder, and salt and mix until well-incorporated.

Drop by spoonfuls onto a parchment-lined baking sheet and bake for 9–12 minutes, or until the edges are lightly browned. Transfer to a cooling rack and let cool completely before glazing.

For the glaze: In a medium saucepan, combine all the ingredients over medium heat. Add just enough water to achieve a pourable consistency. With a paper towel under the cooling rack to catch drips, spoon a fair amount of glaze over each cookie. Let cool completely before storing.

Lemon Cornmeal Cookies

Makes about 15 cookies

These have a lovely unique texture, sort of crunchy and chewy. The taste is mild and lemony, and the sugar coating is the perfect finishing touch.

1 cup flour
½ cup yellow cornmeal
¼ teaspoon salt
1 teaspoon baking powder
½ cup canola oil

½ cup sugar
2 teaspoons lemon zest
2 tablespoons soy milk
½ teaspoon vanilla extract
About ⅓ cup sugar, to coat

Preheat oven to 350°F.

In a medium bowl, combine flour, cornmeal, salt, and baking powder.

Make a well in the middle and add the oil, sugar, zest, soy milk, and vanilla. Mix until well-combined.

The dough will be crumbly but will hold together when formed.

Form into 2-inch disks and flop both sides in sugar.

Place on a parchment-lined baking sheet and bake for 8–10 minutes or until the edges are golden brown, then transfer to a wire cooling rack to cool completely.

Lemon Poppy Seed Cookies

Makes about 25 cookies

While lemon poppy seed cookies sound exotic, they are actually very traditional, like cookies someone's grandma would make . . . if this grandma were a total badass. But that's everyone's grandma, right?

⅓ cup canola oil
⅔ cup sugar
1 tablespoon lemon zest
¼ cup soy milk

1 ⅓ cups flour
1 teaspoon baking powder
¼ teaspoon salt
1 tablespoon poppy seeds

Preheat oven to 350°F.

Stir together the oil and sugar until combined. Add the lemon zest and soy milk and beat until smooth and consistent.

Add the flour, baking powder, salt, and poppy seeds and mix until well-combined. The dough should be spoonable, not stiff.

Drop by heaping teaspoonfuls onto a baking sheet lined with parchment paper (about 2 inches apart), and flatten slightly. Bake for 9–11 minutes, or until the edges are golden brown. Let sit on the baking sheet for about a minute before transferring them to a cooling rack to cool completely.

Sticky Date and Apple Squares

Makes an 8x8-inch pan of squares

These squares are wholesome and delicious, thanks to the generous amount of nuts and fruit in them. So if you find yourself eating half the tray, be unapologetic!

½ cup margarine
½ cup brown sugar
⅓ cup light corn syrup or maple syrup
1 cup chopped dates
2 cups oats

2 cups flour
1 teaspoon baking soda
2 apples, peeled and chopped
2 teaspoons lemon juice
½ cup coarsely chopped walnuts

Preheat oven to 350°F.

In a small saucepan, mix together the margarine, brown sugar, corn syrup, and dates. Stir until the sugar dissolves and the mixture bubbles. Set aside.

In a large bowl, mix together the oats, flour, and baking soda. Pour in the sugar mixture, then add the apples and lemon juice.

Pour into an 8x8-inch pan lined with parchment paper. Top with the walnuts and bake for 12–15 minutes. Cut as desired.

Vanilla Thumbprints

Makes 18 cookies

How could I not include a vanilla variation of the utterly adorable thumbprint cookie? These are similar to a sugar cookie, but with a fudgy texture and a burst of fruit flavor. You can use any kind of jam you like.

⅓ cup canola oil
⅔ cup sugar
¼ cup soy milk
1 teaspoon vanilla extract

1 ¾ cups flour
1 teaspoon baking powder
⅛ teaspoon salt
3–4 tablespoons jam, your choice

Preheat oven to 350°F.

In a medium bowl, mix the oil, sugar, soy milk, and extract.

Sift in the flour, baking powder, and salt and stir until completely mixed. Add a bit more flour if the dough looks wet.

Shape into tablespoon-sized balls and place on a lightly oiled or parchment-lined baking sheet (do not flatten) and bake for 10 minutes.

Remove from oven and, using your thumb, press into each cookie, making a thumbprint. Put about ½ teaspoon jam on each cookie. Return to the oven and bake for 3 more minutes.

Transfer to a wire rack to cool and enjoy!

Bar Cookies

With all the surface area on top, cookie bars have the ability to hold chocolate, frosting, gooey caramel, and more, making them especially decadent. These recipes will take you beyond your basic brownie.

Caramel Apple Bars

Makes an 8x8-inch pan of bars

These bars are soft, sweet squares of apple pie with oozing caramel—an absolutely perfect autumnal treat.

For the apples:

3 medium apples, peeled and chopped

1 tablespoon cornstarch

½ cup brown sugar

3 tablespoons soy milk

½ teaspoon vanilla extract

For the base:

½ cup canola oil

¾ cup brown sugar

3 tablespoons maple syrup

½ teaspoon dark molasses

2 tablespoons applesauce

1 teaspoon vanilla extract

2 ½ cups flour

1 teaspoon baking soda

¼ teaspoon salt

Caramel: Caramel from Caramel Hazelnut Brownies (page 150), minus the hazelnuts

For the apples: Combine the apples, cornstarch, brown sugar, soy milk, and vanilla in a small saucepan over medium heat and stir until the cornstarch and sugar dissolve. Cook until the mixture thickens and the apples are soft, then remove from heat and let cool.

For the base: Preheat oven to 350°F. Grease an 8x8-inch baking pan or line it with parchment. In a large bowl, stir together the oil, sugar, maple syrup, molasses, applesauce, and vanilla. Add the flour, baking soda, and salt and stir until combined. Press the dough into the baking pan and top with the fruit mixture. Bake for 16–20 minutes or until the cookie part is firm and golden. Check a part on the edge where the fruit doesn't cover. Remove from oven and let set.

For the caramel (if using): When the bars are in the oven, prepare according to directions and let cool. When the bars are cooled, drizzle with the caramel and let set.

147

Cherry Pie Bars

Makes an 8x8-inch pan of bars

These bars are really versatile. The caramel-y cookie base is the foundation for infinite pie possibilities, and the cherries can be replaced with any fruit your heart desires.

For the fruit:
2 ½ cups fresh or frozen cherries, chopped (or fruit of your choice)
1 tablespoon cornstarch
½ cup brown sugar
3 tablespoons soy milk
½ teaspoon vanilla extract

For the base:
½ cup canola oil
¾ cup brown sugar
3 tablespoons maple syrup
½ teaspoon dark molasses
2 tablespoons applesauce
1 teaspoon vanilla extract
2 ½ cups flour
1 teaspoon baking soda
¼ teaspoon salt

For the fruit: Combine all ingredients in a small saucepan over medium heat and stir until the cornstarch and sugar dissolve. Cook until the mixture thickens and the cherries are softened, then remove from heat and let cool.

For the base:
Preheat oven to 350°F.
Grease an 8x8-inch baking pan or line it with parchment.
In a large bowl, stir together the oil, sugar, maple syrup, molasses, applesauce, and vanilla. Add the flour, baking soda, and salt and stir until combined.
Press the dough into the baking pan and top with the fruit mixture.
Bake for 16–20 minutes or until the cookie part is firm and golden. Check a part on the edge where the fruit doesn't cover.
Let set and eat!

Caramel Hazelnut Brownie Bars

Makes
9–16 bars,
depending on
how you cut
them

If you like regular brownies, just wait until you try these smothered in caramel and topped with crunchy flavorful hazelnuts.

1 cup raw hazelnuts

For the brownies:

½ cup chocolate chips, melted

⅓ cup canola oil

1 ¼ cups sugar

1 ½ teaspoons vanilla extract

⅓ cup soy milk

1 ½ cups flour

½ cup cocoa powder

1 ½ teaspoons baking powder

½ cup toasted hazelnuts, from below,
    chopped coarsely

For the caramel topping:

⅓ cup soy milk

¼ cup margarine

¾ cup brown sugar

½ teaspoon vanilla extract

2 tablespoons flour

½ cup of the hazelnuts from below,
    halved and quartered

Preheat oven to 400°F.

Place hazelnuts on a cookie tray and toast in the oven for 5–7 minutes until fragrant. Remove most of the skins by rubbing them off in a kitchen towel or between your hands. It's okay if they don't come off completely or some of them don't come off at all.

For the brownies: Preheat oven to 350°F. Stir together the melted chocolate chips, oil, sugar, vanilla, and soy milk in a large bowl. Add the flour, cocoa powder, and baking powder. Stir in the hazelnuts until evenly distributed. Press the dough into a greased or parchment-lined 8x8-inch baking pan. Bake for 22–24 minutes.

For the caramel: While the brownies are baking, make the caramel. In a medium saucepan, stir together the soy milk, margarine, brown sugar, vanilla, and flour. Turn the heat on medium-high and let cook until soft ball stage, stirring frequently. (If a bit of the caramel dropped into a bowl of cold water flattens and holds its shape, but is still soft and pliable, it's at soft ball stage.) Stir in the hazelnuts, pour the caramel into a bowl, and chill until the brownies are done.

Assembly: Let the brownies cool for about 10 minutes, then pour the caramel evenly over the surface. Chill in the freezer for 15–20 minutes, then cut and serve!

Cashew Cappuccino Nanaimo Bars

Makes about 2 dozen bars

These bars are very versatile. Don't have cashews? Make these with walnuts or shredded coconut. Kahlúa is highly recommended for these, but if you don't have any on hand, it can be replaced with another coffee liqueur or coffee extract.

Bottom Layer:
⅓ cup margarine
⅓ cup sugar
½ cup cocoa powder, sifted
⅓ cup soy milk
2 ⅓ cups graham cracker crumbs
⅓ cup cashews, crushed
⅓ cup chocolate chips, melted
2 teaspoons Kahlúa, coffee liqueur, or
    coffee extract

Center:
¼ cup margarine
3 cups powdered sugar
3 tablespoons soy milk
1 teaspoon freshly ground coffee beans
1 teaspoon Kahlúa, coffee liqueur, or
    coffee extract
Topping:
1 cup chocolate chips
1 tablespoon shortening

Preheat oven to 350°F.

Bottom Layer: Cream together the margarine, sugar, cocoa, and soy milk in a large bowl. Stir in the graham cracker crumbs and cashews. Stir in the melted chocolate and Kahlúa. Press evenly into an 8x8-inch brownie pan lined with parchment paper. Bake for 14–15 minutes until firm. Cool. In the meantime, make the filling.

Center: Cream together the margarine, powdered sugar, and soy milk until fluffy. Add the ground coffee and Kahlúa and beat until all is combined.

Topping: Wait until the last minute to make this. Melt the chocolate chips and shortening either in the microwave or in your makeshift double boiler.

Assembly: Spread the filling atop the cooled bottom layer and chill in the fridge for about 15 minutes. Pour and spread the chocolate topping on top of the first two layers. Give the chocolate at least 20 minutes to set at room temperature, then cut and enjoy!

Chocolate-Covered Granola Bars

**Makes
8–10 bars**

So much better than store bought! The granola bar part can be a little sticky on these before you dip them in chocolate, so leave them in the freezer as long as possible.

½ cup sugar
½ cup light brown sugar
1 cup soy milk
2 cups oats
1 tablespoon margarine
½ teaspoon vanilla extract

Chocolate for dipping or drizzling:
1 cup chocolate chips
2 teaspoons shortening

In a small saucepan over medium-high heat, combine the sugars and soy milk and stir until boiling, about 3–4 minutes.

Lower the heat to medium and cook for another 5–7 minutes, stirring frequently.

Add the oats, margarine, and vanilla. Cook until at soft ball stage (235°F). To figure that out, use a candy thermometer or drop a bit of the mixture (or just the liquid if you can get it) into a measuring cup filled with cold water. If it flattens at the bottom of the cup and is soft, but still holds its shape, perfect. If the liquid dissolves, keep cooking the mixture.

Remove from heat and transfer to a small bowl. Let sit for a couple minutes, then add the chocolate chips; be careful so they don't melt into the mixture too much. Form into 8 or so bars and place on parchment-lined cookie sheet. Freeze for at least 30 minutes. Melt the chocolate and shortening together in a makeshift double boiler over the stove. Once melted, coat the granola bars (completely, halfway, drizzled on—however you like). It's easiest to do this with a knife or spoon instead of dipping the bars in the chocolate.

Place the chocolate-coated bars back on the parchment until the chocolate is set, then transfer to an airtight container. It's a good idea to store in the fridge, but not necessary. These are addictive!

Chocolate Peppermint Cream Bars

Makes 2–3 dozen

These are another contender from the 1998 Wisconsin Electric Company Cookie Book, adapted and veganized. Pure chocolate and peppermint bliss! They're not all that difficult or time-consuming either, despite having three layers. Don't be afraid of them, especially if you have a proper kitchen, as I was able to whip up a batch of these for my friend Alexis's birthday in my dorm room/ancient basement kitchen freshman year of art school. They do call for a lot of chocolate chips, but feel free to halve the recipe and make in an 8x4-inch bread pan. Don't wait for the holidays to make these!

Bottom Layer:
1 ¼ cups chocolate chips
½ cup soy milk
⅔ cup cocoa powder
⅓ cup margarine
1 cup sugar

¾ teaspoon vanilla extract
2 scant cups flour
⅛ teaspoon salt
Peppermint Cream:
½ cup margarine
2 ¼ cups powdered sugar

2 teaspoons peppermint extract

3–4 drops green food coloring (optional, but attractive)

2 tablespoons soy milk, plus more if needed

Chocolate Layer:

1 ¼ cups chocolate chips

2 tablespoons shortening

Preheat the oven to 350°F.

Bottom Layer: Melt the chocolate chips either in the microwave or in a glass bowl placed in boiling water. Remove from heat and stir in the soy milk and the cocoa powder. Cream together margarine and sugar with a strong fork, then add the chocolate/soy milk/cocoa mixture and stir until incorporated. Add the vanilla, then the flour and salt. No need to sift.

In an 8x8-inch baking pan *lined with parchment paper* (I cannot stress enough the importance), press out the dough evenly. Bake for 14–18 minutes or until the center is firm and the edges are done, then cool.

Peppermint Cream: Meanwhile, cream together the margarine and powdered sugar. Add the peppermint extract and food coloring (if using). Gradually add the soy milk until the mixture resembles frosting. If it's liquid, add more powdered sugar. If it's stiff or dry, add more soy milk. Chill in the fridge until the bottom layer is cooled.

Chocolate Layer (Make this at the last minute): Melt the chocolate chips and shortening in a glass bowl in boiling water, or over a double boiler.

Assembly: Spread the bottom layer evenly with peppermint cream, then chill in the freezer for about 5 minutes. Remove, then spread the top with the chocolate, creating a swirl pattern if you like. The chocolate will not spread out evenly due to the peppermint layer, but if you want it to be smooth, do a second layer of chocolate, halving the chocolate layer ingredients. Let set, then cut as you like and enjoy!

Sticky Coconut Chocolate Chip Oat Bars

Makes an 8x4-inch pan of bars

These are reminiscent of chocolate chip granola bars with the addition of coconut, but more flavorful and a bit softer.

¼ cup sugar
¼ cup brown sugar
¼ cup soy milk
3 tablespoons maple syrup
1 ½ tablespoons cornstarch
1 ½ tablespoons water
½ teaspoon vanilla
½ teaspoon coconut extract

1 tablespoon margarine
¾ cup sweetened or unsweetened (depending on preference or what you have) flaked coconut
¾ cup oats
3 tablespoons flour
⅓ cup chocolate chips

Preheat oven to 350°F.

In a small saucepan over medium heat, combine the sugars, soy milk, and maple syrup. Cook for 5–6 minutes until the sugar dissolves and the mixture starts to thicken a bit (no need to cook it all the way to soft ball stage).

Dissolve the cornstarch in the water in a small bowl, then add to the saucepan and cook for 2–3 more minutes until thick. Remove from heat, then add the vanilla, coconut extract, margarine, coconut, oats, and flour. Stir.

Transfer mixture into an 8x4-inch baking pan lined with parchment paper, sprinkle the chocolate chips evenly over the top, and stir them in a little bit. Bake for 14–16 minutes until golden brown, let cool in the pan, then cut and serve!

Orange Vanilla Dream Bars

Makes 16–36 bars, depending on how you cut them

These orange cream bars are a slice of a pastel, surreal dream. The tops are citrusy and creamy and the vanilla bottoms appropriately delicate.

½ cup margarine
½ cup sugar
⅓ cup powdered sugar
¾ teaspoon vanilla extract
2 tablespoons orange marmalade
3 tablespoons orange juice
2 ⅔ cups flour
1 teaspoon baking powder
⅛ teaspoon salt

Cream:
¼ cup shortening
2 tablespoons margarine
1 ½ teaspoons orange extract
¼ teaspoon vanilla extract
1 tablespoon orange juice
1 tablespoon soy milk
1 tablespoon orange marmalade
2 ¾ cups powdered sugar
Orange food coloring (optional)

Preheat oven to 350°F.

Line an 8x8-inch baking pan with parchment paper and set aside. In a large bowl, cream together the margarine, sugar, and powdered sugar until smooth. Add the vanilla, orange marmalade, and orange juice. Sift in the flour, baking powder, and salt, and mix until just combined. Press the dough evenly into the parchment-lined pan and bake for 16 minutes, or until golden. Let cool on a wire rack. In the meantime, make the orange cream.

For the cream: In a medium bowl, cream together the shortening and margarine. Add the orange extract, vanilla, orange juice, soy milk, and orange marmalade and beat until smooth.

Gradually sift in the powdered sugar until all is incorporated. The mixture should be thicker than normal frosting, but not crumbly. If it's too wet, add a bit more powdered sugar, and if it's crumbly, add a splash of soy milk.

Assembly: When the bottom is completely cool, spread the cream atop it, evenly, smoothing it out completely with a spatula. Chill in the fridge until the cream is firm, then cut into bars. Any size is fine, but they look especially cute cut into small rectangles.

Peanut Butter Chocolate-Covered Pretzel Bars

Makes about 8 bars, depending on how they're cut

Peanut butter bars! Chocolate-covered pretzels! Chocolate-covered peanuts! All in one bar! Perfect for when you want sweet, salty, and chocolate all in one bite.

1 ½ cups chocolate chips
2 teaspoons shortening
About 36 mini pretzels, preferably salted
½ cup roasted peanuts
½ cup peanut butter
¾ cup brown sugar
1 tablespoon peanut oil
¼ cup soy milk

2 tablespoons maple syrup
¾ teaspoon vanilla extract
1 ¼ cups flour
½ teaspoon baking powder
½ teaspoon baking soda
⅛ teaspoon salt
Handful of chocolate chips

Start by dipping the pretzels and peanuts.
In a glass bowl in a pan of boiling water over the stove, melt the chocolate chips and shortening.

Dip all the pretzels first, dropping them in the chocolate, then removing with a fork and letting the excess chocolate drip off.

Transfer pretzels to parchment paper on a plate or cookie sheet. Don't spread them out too much; it's okay if they stick together.

After all the pretzels are dipped, pour the peanuts into the chocolate bowl and stir until coated, then drop onto the parchment with the pretzels.

Let harden at room temperature.

Preheat oven to 350°F.

In a large bowl, mix the peanut butter, brown sugar, oil, soy milk, maple syrup, and vanilla. Stir until smooth.

Sift in the flour, baking powder, baking soda, and salt.

Press dough into an 8x8-inch baking pan lined with parchment paper. Bake for 16–18 minutes, until firm. Don't worry if it seems a bit doughy; the peanut butter layer is a bit gooey rather than cakelike.

Once the peanut butter bars are out of the oven, let cool for 5 minutes while you break up the chocolate-covered pretzels and peanuts in pieces (the size of ½ a pretzel or less).

Scatter the pretzels, peanuts, and chocolate chips evenly over the top of the bars. Let sit until they look melty, then press down a bit. At this point, stick the pan in the freezer until the chocolate hardens up again. This is to prevent the pretzels from sitting out too long and getting soggy. This way, they'll stay crunchy. Remove pan from freezer, then cut and enjoy!

S'mores Bars

**Makes 9–16
squares,
depending on
how you cut
them**

Indoor s'mores in cookie form! The trick to browning the marshmallows is using your oven's broiler. Vegan marshmallows are pretty easy to find these days in health food stores or online.

1 batch Graham Cracker dough (page 106)
1 cup chocolate chips
2 cups vegan marshmallows, cut into fourths OR vegan marshmallow cream

Preheat oven to 350°F.

Prepare the graham cracker dough according to its instructions, then press into an 8x8-inch baking pan lined with parchment and bake for 18–20 minutes, until the bars are firm and golden brown.

Remove from oven and immediately scatter the chocolate chips evenly over the surface. When they start to get melty, spread them around with a knife. Set aside.

Preheat your oven's broiler to 500°F.

Scatter the marshmallows (or dollop on marshmallow cream, if using) over the surface of the bars and put under the broiler for about 3 minutes until they turn golden. Rotate the pan if necessary. Don't let them get too melty, though.

Remove from oven and let cool, then cut and devour!

Alternatively, if you want to make s'mores with crispy graham crackers, make the graham crackers, let cool, and break into squares. Melt the chocolate chips and spread some chocolate on half the graham cracker squares. Place a half or whole marshmallow atop each of the chocolaty halves and put under the 500°F broiler on a cookie sheet until the marshmallow turns golden. Place the other graham cracker halves on the marshmallows and eat!

Seven-Layer Bars

Makes an
8x8-inch pan
of bars

Contrary to their name, these bars don't really have seven layers, but they're really good and super easy to make! If you have trouble finding vegan butterscotch chips, you can just add more chocolate chips or white chocolate chips.

Crust:
½ cup margarine, melted
3 tablespoons agave nectar
2 cups graham cracker crumbs, store bought or homemade (page 106)
Coconut Caramel:
3 tablespoons soy milk

2 tablespoons margarine
⅓ cup brown sugar
¼ teaspoon vanilla extract
¼ tablespoon coconut extract
1 tablespoon flour
Layers:
1 cup chocolate chips
Coconut Caramel

½ cup unsweetened coconut (optional, but recommended)
⅔–¾ cup butterscotch chips
1 cup walnuts (or almonds, pecans, etc.), chopped

Preheat oven to 350°F.

Prepare an 8x8-inch baking pan with parchment paper and set aside.

In a medium bowl, mix together all the crust ingredients, then press evenly in the prepared pan with a spatula.

Make the coconut caramel: In a medium saucepan, stir together the soy milk, margarine, brown sugar, vanilla, coconut extract, and flour. Turn the heat on medium-high and let cook until soft ball stage, stirring frequently. If a bit of the caramel dropped into a bowl of cold water flattens and holds its shape, it's at soft boil. Stir in half the coconut.

Scatter the chocolate chips evenly over the surface of the crust, then pour the coconut caramel over the top, sprinkle the rest of the coconut, scatter the butterscotch chips, and finish by topping with the chopped walnuts.

Press down on the unbaked bars with the spatula, then bake for 15 minutes or until the crust looks and feels firm and the chocolate is melted.

Let them sit in the pan until almost completely cooled so they hold together, then cut and transfer to a plate. Store in an airtight container.

A Take on Tradition

This chapter covers traditional cookies enjoyed all over the world and some basic holiday cookies. Enjoy these cookies by the fireplace with a cup of hot chocolate or tea.

Biscotti: Two Basic Recipes

Makes 24 biscotti

These recipes will make basic plain biscotti and chocolate biscotti, but don't be fooled into thinking they're boring; the possibilities for variations are endless. The variations are fairly interchangeable with each kind of biscotti, so feel free to mix and match.

Plain biscotti:
½ cup margarine
¾ cup sugar
¼ cup soy milk
½ teaspoon vanilla extract
2 cups flour
1 ½ teaspoons baking powder
¼ teaspoon salt
Chocolate biscotti:

½ cup margarine
1 cup sugar
¼ cup soy milk
½ teaspoon vanilla extract
¼ teaspoon almond extract
1 ½ cups flour
½ cup cocoa powder
1 ½ teaspoons baking powder
¼ teaspoon salt

Preheat oven to 325°F.

For plain biscotti: Cream together the margarine, sugar, soy milk, and vanilla with an electric mixer. Add the flour, baking powder, and salt.

Form dough into a 3-inch wide and 1-inch thick loaf and bake on a parchment-lined or lightly greased cookie sheet for 30 minutes.

Let cool for 10–15 minutes, then slice into ½-inch wedges and bake for 5 more minutes on each side.

For chocolate biscotti: Cream together the margarine, sugar, soy milk, and extracts with an electric mixer. Add the flour, cocoa, baking powder, and salt.

Form dough into a 3-inch wide and 1-inch thick loaf and bake on a parchment-lined or lightly greased cookie sheet for 30 minutes. Let cool for 10–15 minutes, then slice into ½-inch wedges and bake for 5 more minutes on each side.

VARIATIONS:

Citrus Biscotti: Add 1 teaspoon of lemon or orange zest to the vanilla biscotti when you add the soy milk. Orange biscotti would also taste wonderful dipped in chocolate.

Chocolate Dipped Biscotti: Melt ¾ cup chocolate chips with ½ teaspoon shortening. Dip your cooled biscotti in the chocolate, place on parchment paper, and let the chocolate set at room temperature.

Chocolate Chip Biscotti: Add ⅓ cup chocolate chips when you add the flour.

Mocha Biscotti: Add 3 tablespoons freshly ground coffee when you add the soy milk.

Nutty Biscotti: Add ⅓ cup chopped roasted nuts, any kind, when you add the flour.

Hazelnut Biscotti: Replace 1 tablespoon of the soy milk with hazelnut liqueur and add ⅓ cup chopped roasted hazelnuts when you add the flour.

Chocolate Mocha Nut Biscotti: Add 3 tablespoons freshly ground coffee and 1 teaspoon coffee liqueur (optional) when you add the soy milk, and ⅓ cup chocolate chips and ⅓ cup almonds or cashews when you add the flour. Dip in or drizzle with chocolate.

Ginger Biscotti: Add ⅓ cup chopped crystallized ginger when you add the flour. Dip in chocolate if you like.

Cranberry Pecan Biscotti: Add ½ teaspoon orange extract with the vanilla and ¼ cup each chopped pecans and dried cranberries when you add the flour.

Candy Cane Chocolate Chip Cookies

Makes 2 dozen

These incredibly chewy peppermint-flavored cookies are scattered with chocolate chips and studded with bits of crushed candy canes. They are the perfect holiday cookie, but certainly can be enjoyed any time of year. The simplest way to crush the candy canes is in a plastic baggie with a hammer. These cookies don't really brown, so don't worry if they look under baked when you take them out of the oven. Plus, the pale cookies with red candy cane bits look festive!

½ cup canola oil
1 ½ cups sugar
½ cup soy milk
1 teaspoon vanilla extract
¾ teaspoon peppermint extract
3 cups flour

1 teaspoon baking powder
¼ teaspoon salt
8 candy canes, crushed (yields about ½ cup)
⅔ cup chocolate chips

Preheat oven to 350°F.

In a large bowl, stir together the canola oil, sugar, soy milk, vanilla, and peppermint extract.

Sift in the flour, baking powder, and salt. Stir in the candy canes and chocolate chips. Add a splash of soy milk if the dough is dry or won't hold together.

Drop by spoonfuls, about two tablespoons each, onto a parchment-lined cookie sheet and flatten. The parchment is very important because if you don't use it, the candy canes will melt and harden on the cookie sheet. You'll spend hours scraping it off. Use parchment! Bake for 8–10 minutes until golden around the edges and firm in the middle. Take out of the oven and immediately transfer to a wire cooling rack very carefully.

English Toffee Squares

*Makes 25
squares*

These cookies are an old family recipe that I veganized. They are super addictive! This recipe can be halved and baked in an 8x4-inch loaf pan, if you wish.

½ cup margarine
⅔ cup brown sugar
¾ teaspoon vanilla extract
1 ⅓ cups flour
1 cup chocolate chips
⅔ cup chopped nuts (almonds, walnuts, or a mixture)

Preheat oven to 350°F.

Cream together the margarine and brown sugar with electric beaters. Add the vanilla. Gradually sift in the flour and stir until incorporated. Press dough into an 8x8-inch nonstick (parchment-lined) baking pan and bake for about 15 minutes until firm and golden. Don't take them out too early or they won't get crispy and toffee-like.

Remove from oven and uniformly sprinkle the chocolate chips in the pan. Return to the oven for about 30 seconds so the chocolate is melty and spreadable. Using a knife, spread the chocolate evenly over the cookie layer. Sprinkle with the nuts, then let cool so the chocolate firms up. Cut into 25 squares and transfer to a cooling rack. Enjoy!

Fortune and Flute Cookies

Makes 12–15 cookies

These cookies are very delicate—perfecting them is a process of trial and error. Bake them too long and they will crack; bake them not long enough and they won't hold their shape. The end result, however, is a delightfully crispy cookie that is worth the experimentation.

⅓ cup soy milk
2 teaspoons cornstarch
2 tablespoons margarine
½ cup powdered sugar

1 teaspoon vanilla extract
½ cup flour
Small strips of paper with fortunes
    written on them

Preheat oven to 375°F.

Dissolve the soy milk in the cornstarch in a small bowl (if microwaving) or in a small saucepan. Heat in the microwave or over medium heat on the stove top until thickened.

Add the margarine to the soy milk/cornstarch mixture and stir until melted. Let cool.

Add the powdered sugar, vanilla, and flour. Stir until emulsified.

For fortune cookies, drop a small spoonful of batter onto a parchment-lined baking sheet and spread out as thinly as possible into a 3-inch diameter circle with your finger. The edges should be thicker than the centers because the edges will bake faster and if the centers are too thick, they won't hold their shape. Only make 3 or 4 at a time, because they cool quickly when they come out of the oven, and you don't want them to crisp up before you fold them.

For flute cookies (straw cookies, pirouettes), you'll need wooden chopsticks to roll them around when they come out of the oven. Have those ready. The same principles apply for these cookies, but you'll want to spread the dough out into a 2-inch-wide rectangle with the length a little less than the length of a chopstick. Again, only make a few at a time.

Have shot glasses or wineglasses with a small diameter ready for when the cookies come out of the oven. They'll be used to hold the shape of the cookies while they cool.

Bake for 5 minutes (you'll find the right time with experimentation, but 5 minutes seems to be the magic number for my oven), until just the edges are golden brown. Take the cookie tray out of the oven and immediately flip all the cookies upside down.

Place your fortunes in the centers of the cookies and loosely fold in half over the strips of paper, then fold lengthwise and immediately place on a shot glass, fold down, so that they hold their shape as they cool.

To create a strawlike cookie, place your chopsticks on the long edges of the rectangles and roll around the chopstick. Place seam-side down on top of a shot glass and let cool.

If desired, fill the flute cookies with Chocolate Buttercream (page 267) by using a small piping tip. Drizzle with chocolate.

If they don't turn out crispy for you the first time around, salvage the cookies by filling them with Buttercream (page 267) and sprinkling with chocolate shavings for pseudo cannoli. Ooh!

Gingerbread Cutout Cookies

Makes 15–30 cookies, depending on size

These are very traditional gingerbread people cookies in theory, but you can decorate them any crazy way you like!

½ cup canola oil
¾ cup brown sugar
¼ cup sugar
¼ cup dark molasses
⅓ cup soy milk
2 ½ cups flour
½ teaspoon baking powder

¾ teaspoon powdered ginger
½ teaspoon cinnamon
⅛ teaspoon ground cloves
⅛ teaspoon allspice
Icing:
1 cup powdered sugar
2 teaspoons soy milk

In a large bowl, stir together the oil, sugars, molasses, and soy milk.

Add the flour, baking soda, ginger, cinnamon, cloves, and allspice, and mix until everything is combined.

Collect the dough into a ball, wrap it in plastic or parchment paper, and chill for at least an hour.

Preheat oven to 350°F.

Roll out the dough (in two or three portions) and cut out with gingerbread people cookie cutters or whatever shapes you like. Make thin cookies if you want them to be crispy or thick if you want soft and chewy.

Transfer to a parchment-lined cookie sheet and bake for 12 minutes (for crispy) or 9 minutes (for soft and chewy).

Transfer to a wire rack to cool, then ice if you like.

In a plastic baggie, mix together the powdered sugar and soy milk, then cut off one of the corners and ice!

Care Packages: Don't Let Your Cookies Crumble

A care package full of cookies can certainly make someone's day, but the sentiment is even sweeter if the cookies arrive fresh and in one piece. Of course, some cookies travel better than others, so here are some dos and don'ts for mailing cookies:

1. Don't send anything chocolate-covered when it's hot outside. I'm sure you can imagine what will happen.
2. Don't send really delicate cookies (like Fortune and Flute Cookies) because they will probably break, regardless of how carefully you package them.
3. Don't send anything that's gooey, caramel-y, or has a fruit sauce. It will be a huge mess and melt like crazy.
4. Do send sturdy cookies that will hold up well and won't break. I've had success with sending Double Peanut Butter Sandwich Cookies (page 104) and Chocolate Peppermint Wafer Cookies (page 122). Even though they contain peanut butter filling and are chocolate-covered, respectively, they hold up well if it's not hot outside.
5. Do package your cookies in small containers lined with paper towels for padding, then place in a slightly larger packaging box. Wrap in brown paper (paper grocery bags work well) if you like, then tape securely.
6. Do place a slice of bread wrapped in a napkin in the container with your cookies if you're worried about them drying out. Just don't include crispy cookies in the same package because the bread will make them soggy.
7. Do let the post office employees know you're sending cookies that are fragile.
8. Do package conservatively. Try to fit as many cookies as you can in the smallest containers possible. Large packages can get expensive to ship.

Jam Kolaches

Makes 2–3 dozen

These traditional Polish cookies rely on cream cheese for flavor, so directly substituting vegan cream cheese works beautifully. Even though they are fancy-looking, they're quite simple to make. I've also included a variation for Poppy Seed Rugelach, a suggestion from my tester, Caitlin.

½ cup margarine

3 ounces (a heaping ⅓ cup) vegan cream cheese

1 ¼ cups flour

¼ cup jam, any flavor

About ¼ cup powdered sugar

Preheat oven to 375°F.

Beat together the margarine and cream cheese with an electric mixer until smooth. Sift in the flour and stir until incorporated. Don't mix too much or the dough might be a bit gummy.

Roll the dough ⅛-inch thick on a floured counter (if you're having trouble with the dough being sticky, pop it in the freezer for 10–15 minutes).

Cut 2-inch circles out of the dough with a glass, cup, or cookie cutter with a 2-inch diameter. If you can't find anything, a knife works fine, too, but it's a little more time-consuming.

Plop a heaping ¼ teaspoon jam in the center of each circle. It's tempting to add more, but it will melt all over the cookie and onto the tray when baked (personal experience!).

Fold two opposite sides of each cookie to the middle so that the edges touch.

Bake for 13–15 minutes or until firm, then remove from the oven and sprinkle with the powdered sugar, preferably using a sifter to make them look pretty.

Transfer to a cooling rack and eat!

Poppy Seed Rugelach Variation: Mix together 3 tablespoons poppy seeds, 3 tablespoons sugar, and ¼ teaspoon ground ginger. Divide dough into 3 portions. Take one portion and roll out into a 7-inch circle (make the circle as perfect as possible, using a knife to fix it) on a floured surface. Sprinkle a third of the poppy seed mixture evenly on top and press down lightly. Cut like a pizza into 12 triangles. Roll up the triangles, starting from the wide side, and bake as directed in the recipe.

Kourabiedes

These traditional Greek cookies are flavored with orange flower water, an ingredient that can be found in Middle Eastern markets and some grocery stores. They are very elegant—perfect for a fancy tea party.

⅓ cup margarine
½ cup powdered sugar
2 teaspoons orange flower water
⅛ teaspoon ground nutmeg

¾ cup flour
¾ cup ground almonds
¼ cup toasted, chopped almonds

Preheat oven to 325°F.

Cream together the margarine and powdered sugar until smooth. Add the orange flower water and ground nutmeg. Sift in the flour and stir until combined. Add the ground and chopped almonds and mix until completely incorporated.

Take 2-teaspoon portions of dough and roll into logs, then shape into crescents. Place crescents on a parchment-lined baking sheet and bake for 12–14 minutes. Remove from the oven and let cool on the tray for a few minutes, then sprinkle some powdered sugar atop the cookies with a sifter and transfer to a wire rack to cool.

Mexican Wedding Cookies

Makes 20 or so cookies

This traditional cookie goes vegan! If you never find yourself at a wedding in Mexico, it's okay to make these anywhere and anytime you're in the mood.

⅔ cup margarine
1 ½ cups powdered sugar
1 teaspoon vanilla extract
1 ½ tablespoons soy milk

⅛ teaspoon salt
2 cups flour
¾ cup pecans, crushed
Extra powdered sugar for sprinkling

Preheat oven to 375°F.

Cream together the margarine and powdered sugar with electric beaters in a medium-large bowl. Add the vanilla, soy milk, and salt. Gradually sift in the flour, stirring after each addition, then dump in the pecans and incorporate them into the mixture.

Roll into balls about two tablespoons each, place on a parchment-lined cookie sheet, and bake for 12 minutes. Let sit on the cookie tray for a few minutes, then sprinkle on some powdered sugar with a sifter.

Transfer to a cooling rack.

Rum Balls

Makes about 2 dozen

Watch out—these are addictive and have quite a kick to them. They taste best after a couple days when the flavors have had a chance to meld.

1 cup finely chopped pecans or walnuts
2 cups Vanilla Wafer (page 124) crumbs
1 ¾ cups powdered sugar
¼ cup cocoa

2 tablespoons corn syrup or brown rice syrup
¼ cup rum
½ cup powdered sugar

Combine the nuts and cookie crumbs in a food processor and pulse until chopped finely and combined.

Add the powdered sugar, cocoa, corn syrup, and rum and continue to pulse until the mixture holds together. Add more crumbs and powdered sugar if the mixture looks soupy or add more rum if it's too dry.

Roll into 1-inch balls and roll in the powdered sugar. Store in the refrigerator.

Spritz Cookies

Makes several dozen

My family never made spritz cookies when I was growing up, but one day I came across a cookie press at the thrift store down the street from my house, cleaned it thoroughly, and began experimenting. Making a proper spritz cookie has a lot to do with the temperature of the dough, because if you chill it too long, it'll be difficult to squeeze it out of the press, but if you don't chill it long enough, it won't be thick enough.

1 cup margarine
½ cup sugar
½ teaspoon vanilla extract

1 tablespoon soy milk
2 ¼ cups flour
¼ teaspoons salt

Preheat oven to 350°F.

In a large bowl, cream the margarine, sugar, vanilla, and soy milk with electric beaters. Add the flour, salt, and any optional ingredients. Beat until a dough forms. Make cookies using a cookie press according to the manufacturer's instructions. Bake for 6–8 minutes and transfer to a wire rack to cool.

VARIATIONS:

Chocolate: Replace ¼ cup of the flour with cocoa powder and add ½ teaspoon almond extract with the vanilla.

Lemon: Replace the vanilla with 2 teaspoons lemon zest.

Maple Nut: Replace the vanilla with 1 ½ teaspoons maple extract. Sprinkle chopped nuts atop the cookies before you bake them (but not before they're on the baking sheet, because you won't be able to get them through the press once the nuts are added).

Raspberry Coconut: Replace the vanilla with 1 ½ teaspoons coconut extract and add 3 tablespoons jam when you add the sugar.

Colorful: Knead any color of food colorings into portions of the dough before chilling. Press one at a time or layer the doughs in the cookie press for a tie-dye effect.

Zesty Coconut Lime Wedding Cookies

Makes about 2 dozen

These cookies have the texture and buttery flavor of Mexican wedding cookies with the complementary flavors of coconut and lime. Eating these cookies is a real experience—first they crumble, delivering their rich buttery flavor, then they melt in your mouth and the coconut lime kicks in. I made these for a party in my Spanish class junior year of high school and can confirm they are coconut-hater approved—which is pretty awesome considering they are loaded with coconut and flavored with coconut extract.

1 ¼ cups margarine
½ cup powdered sugar
½ teaspoon vanilla extract
½ teaspoon coconut extract
2 tablespoons lime juice
¾ teaspoon lime zest
1 ¼ cups cornstarch
1 ½ cups flour

¾ cup sweetened flaked coconut
⅔ cup sweetened flaked coconut for
    rolling and sprinkling
Lime glaze:
2 tablespoons lime juice
½ cup powdered sugar
¼ teaspoon coconut extract

Preheat oven to 375°F.

Cream the margarine, powdered sugar, vanilla, coconut extract, lime juice, and lime zest in a large bowl until smooth. Gradually add the cornstarch and flour, beating after each addition, then stir in the coconut, kneading it in, if necessary. If the dough is crumbling, add a touch more lime juice or a splash of soy milk. Roll dough into balls, about 2 tablespoons each.

Pour the coconut into a small bowl, then roll each cookie in the coconut and place on a parchment-lined cookie sheet. Sprinkle the rest of the coconut on top of the cookies.

Bake cookies for about 15 minutes or until they are firm and the bottoms are golden brown. Let sit on the cookie tray for at least 10 minutes before moving to a cooling rack, or they will crumble when you transfer them.

Make the glaze! Combine all ingredients in a small bowl and stir until smooth.

When the cookies are almost completely cooled, dip each one in the glaze and let sit until the glaze dries.

Optional: Sprinkle a bit of green sugar on top of each cookie.

Healthier Cookies and Baking for Specific Needs

There's no reason vegans with allergies and gluten-free vegans should not enjoy fabulous cookies, too! While I'm not an expert on gluten-free baking, I experimented a lot and came up with a few basic recipes so everyone can have vegan cookies. In this section is information about making cookies throughout this book lower-fat, healthier, safe for vegans with allergies, and more. And I could never forget to include a recipe for our furry-legged friends!

How to Make a Cookie Recipe Lower Fat

Blasphemy! Cookies, by nature, are hardly low fat, but I can tell you how to make them so if you must know. The result of these substitutions will be cakier cookies, because margarine and oil create the chewy, crispy, and decadent factors.

Start by omitting half the margarine or oil (omitting more than that or all of it will make the cookies less than desirable).

If the recipe uses margarine, replace half the omitted amount with applesauce, soy yogurt, or soy milk/cornstarch goo (page 216). Be creative and use a replacement that really complements the recipe, such as chocolate pudding in a chocolate cookie or applesauce in a cookie with fruit. Add soy milk if necessary to make the dough the right consistency.

If the recipe uses oil, continue with the recipe as directed and add splashes of soy milk, if necessary, to replace lost moisture. Since oil is so liquid, replacing it with something that has a texture is unnecessary and may make the final product cakier.

Good candidates for a makeover:

Glazed Apple Cider Cookies (page 14)
Chai Cookies (page 17)
Spicy Mexican Hot Chocolate Cookies (page 25)
Root Beer Float Cookies (page 30)
Glazed Rum Raisin Cookies (page 32)
PB&J Thumbprints (page 38)
Soft Peanut Butter Chocolate Chip Cookies (page 41)
Almond Butter Cookies (page 61)
Cranberry Almond Cookies (page 73)
Chocolate Jam Thumbprints (page 88)
Apricot Almond Cookies (page 129)

Autumn Clouds Pumpkin Chocolate Chip Cookies (page 126)
Soft Baked Chocolate Chip Cookies (page 213)
Soft and Delicious Oatmeal Cookies (page 222)
Chewy Spiced Molasses Cookies (page 229)
Snickerdoodles (page 230)

It's generally not a good idea to try to decrease the fat in crispy cookies (Examples: Thin and Crispy Peanut Butter Cookies, page 52; Crispy Pinwheel Cookies with Pink Sugar, page 234), delicate cookies (Examples: Apricot Foldovers, page 242; Chewy Banana-Banana Cookies, page 130), or cookies that have to be rolled out (Examples: Chocolate-Vanilla Hypnosis Cookies, page 250; Cinnamon Roll Cookies, page 246). Using margarine is very important to the texture of crispy, delicate cookies and for holding together cookie dough when rolled. I haven't made each and every one of these recipes low fat to compare to the original version, so feel free to experiment to your heart's content.

How to Make Cookies Healthier with Whole Grains

White flour can be replaced with whole wheat pastry flour, a light and airy flour. It mustn't be confused with regular whole wheat flour, which should never be used in baked goods (other than bread) because it contains more gluten and makes the final product dense with a strong wheat flavor. It's up to you how much you want to replace. Replacing all the white flour will make your cookies denser and will probably give them a bit of a wheat-y flavor, so replacing half is usually best.

You can also use spelt flour, but it's best to only replace half the white flour, because spelt flour is a bit tricky to work with and can make cookies crumble easily. Spelt is in the wheat family and is NOT gluten-free, so spelt flour is not suitable for people who are allergic to wheat or gluten. If you are baking for someone who is gluten-free, consider replacing flour with a gluten-free baking mix, available at most supermarkets, or browse online or at your library to learn more about gluten-free baking.

Some cookies that are delicate in flavor won't taste very good if you replace the all-purpose flour with whole wheat, like Amazingly Soft Sugar Cookies (page 217), Mexican Wedding Cookies (page 185), or Apricot Foldovers (page 242).

How to Ditch the Sugar

Sugar provides sweetness and is an important element in the structural backbone of a cookie, so omitting sugar completely will yield less than desirable results. Fortunately, you can cut down on the sugar a little bit without compromising flavor. Start by using ¼ less sugar and see how you like it. Omitting a lot of sugar can make your cookies taste like health food (in a bad way).

Also, 1 cup of sugar can be replaced with ⅔ cup light agave nectar. Agave is still sugar and contains just as many calories. However, the body digests it differently, making it safe for some people who have sugar sensitivities. Be sure to find out beforehand if it's okay to use if you're baking for someone who avoids regular sugar. Replacing all the sugar in a recipe with agave will mess with the texture a lot, so start off by replacing half and cutting down on the amount of liquid. It's all about experimentation.

Baking for Vegans with Allergies

Baking for someone with allergies on top of baking vegan can be a bit of a challenge, but it's doable with substitutions, patience, and a little experimentation.

If your vegan is soy-free . . .

Replace soy milk with any other kind of nondairy milk.

A lot of margarines have soy products in them, so opt for recipes that use oil or replace the margarine with oil (page 110). Also, Earth Balance makes a soy-free margarine.

Chocolate chips often contain soy lecithin as a stabilizer, so be aware and read labels. It's only a small amount, so check and see how serious the allergy is.

If your vegan is allergic to nuts or peanuts . . .

Simply put, steer clear of Chapter Three!

Replace ground almonds with flour and peanut oil with an oil that won't be an allergy trigger, such as corn or canola oil.

If your vegan is gluten-free . . .

Check out Gluten-Free Chocolate Chip Cookies (page 204).

Replace flour with a gluten-free baking mix.

See what your vegan uses to bake with or study up on gluten-free baking and experiment with flour combinations.

Blueberry Walnut Breakfast Cookies

Makes about 10 cookies

I know you eat cookies for breakfast anyway, so these blueberry cookies, reminiscent of muffin tops, are a wholesome morning treat. They are super good for you, but don't taste healthy in a bad way at all.

⅓ cup soy milk
¾ teaspoon apple cider vinegar
1 cup all-purpose flour
¼ cup whole wheat pastry flour
½ cup oats
1 teaspoon baking powder
1 teaspoon cinnamon

¼ teaspoon salt
¼ cup turbinado sugar
2 tablespoons maple syrup
½ teaspoon vanilla
½ cup fresh blueberries
⅓ cup walnuts (optional)

Preheat oven to 350°F.

Mix the soy milk and vinegar and let sit for 5 minutes.

In a medium bowl, mix together all the dry ingredients, then add the soy milk and vinegar mixture, maple syrup, vanilla, blueberries, and walnuts.

Drop 3-tablespoon portions of dough onto a parchment-lined baking sheet and bake for 12 minutes. Transfer to a wire rack and let cool. These are best eaten right after baking because they tend to get a bit wet and gummy after sitting around for hours.

Coconut Oatmeal Raisin Breakfast Cookies

Makes 8–10 large cookies

These satisfying cookies are healthy, sweetened only with dates and a bit of maple syrup, making them the ideal morning treat while on the go.

1 ½ cups old-fashioned or regular rolled oats

½ cup whole wheat pastry flour

⅓ cup dried, sweetened coconut (flaked or shredded)

¾ teaspoon baking powder

¼ teaspoon baking soda

⅛ teaspoon salt

¾ teaspoon cinnamon

⅓ cup applesauce

⅓ cup soy milk or coconut milk

½ teaspoon dark molasses

¾ teaspoon vanilla extract

1 tablespoon maple syrup

1 tablespoon ground flaxseeds

1 teaspoon canola oil

½ cup dates plus 1 tablespoon hot water

⅓ cup raisins

Preheat oven to 350°F.

In a large bowl, stir together the oats, flour, coconut, baking powder, baking soda, salt, and cinnamon.

Add the applesauce, soy milk, molasses, vanilla, maple syrup, flaxseeds, and canola oil.

Pit and coarsely chop the dates. Combine the dates and hot water in a food processor and blend until smooth. It's okay if you can't get the dates perfectly smooth; some chunks are fine.

Add the date puree to the rest of the ingredients and stir until incorporated.

Stir in the raisins.

Drop by very large spoonfuls onto a cookie sheet lined with parchment paper and bake for about 12–15 minutes until the centers are firm and the edges are golden brown.

"Throw a Bunch of Stuff in a Bowl" Oatmeal Breakfast Bars

Makes an 8x8-inch tray of bars

I make a variation of these bars for breakfast every few weekends. They're easy, nutritious, portable, and delicious! It's a very forgiving recipe and can be varied in so many ways. They can also be made wheat-free if you choose.

3 ¼ cups oats

¾ cup ground oats, spelt flour, or whole wheat pastry flour

1 teaspoon baking powder

1 ½ tablespoons ground flaxseed

½ cup applesauce

1 cup soy milk

¼ cup maple syrup, agave, or brown sugar

1 ½ teaspoons blackstrap molasses

½ teaspoon vanilla

Any or many of the following:

1 cup fresh or frozen berries or fruit (chopped if they're in big pieces)

¾ cup of one of or a mixture of raisins, dried fruit, chocolate chips, nuts, and seeds

2 tablespoons peanut butter, other nut butter, or fruit preserves

Cereal or turbinado sugar for sprinkling on top before baking

Preheat oven to 350°F.

In a large bowl, combine all the ingredients and optional ingredients you are using. Stir until completely combined, then press into a greased 8x8-inch pan and bake for 20–25 minutes or until firm. Cool for a few minutes, then cut!

Peanut Butter Dog Treats

Makes about 3 dozen, depending on size

No cookie book would be complete without dog cookies! Humans can eat them too, although the strong taste of whole wheat flour and the absence of sugar may be an acquired taste for the vegan cookie connoisseur. They will keep for 4–5 days in an airtight container, but will keep for months in the freezer!

1 ½ cups whole wheat flour
1 cup oats
⅓ cup peanut butter

¾ cup warm water
¼ cup chopped peanuts (optional)

In a large bowl, combine the flour and oats. Stir in spoonfuls of the peanut butter one at a time, then pour in the warm water. Stir until combined, then add the peanuts if using.

Wrap dough in plastic wrap and chill in the freezer for 30–40 minutes.

Preheat oven to 300°F.

Shape 2-teaspoon pieces of dough into little bones or just little logs if you're running short on time. Place on a greased cookie sheet.

Bake for 20 minutes, then turn over and bake for another 20 minutes until firm and crunchy. They will harden up a bit once they cool, so don't worry if they don't firm up "enough."

Cool on the tray (don't give them to your pup when they're steaming hot!), store in an airtight container at room temperature for a few days, then transfer to the freezer so they don't go bad.

Gluten-Free Chocolate Chip Cookies

Makes 20 cookies

I wanted to include a chocolate chip cookie recipe for gluten-free vegans to enjoy while still staying true to my belief in the importance of user-friendly recipes and accessible ingredients. So, all the ingredients for these cookies can be found at any supermarket and the cookies are super easy to make.

Don't substitute brown rice flour for the white rice flour, because it will add an undesirable grittiness to the cookies. Check out the Chinese or Indian section of your favorite grocery store, where you can often find some great and relatively inexpensive white rice flour.

½ cup sugar
¼ cup brown sugar
⅓ cup canola oil
1 teaspoon vanilla extract
2 tablespoons soy milk
1 cup white rice flour

⅓ cup soy flour
¼ cup cornstarch
1 teaspoon baking powder
½ teaspoon baking soda
¼ teaspoon salt
¾ cup chocolate chips

Preheat oven to 350°F.

In a medium-large bowl, mix together the sugars, oil, vanilla, and soy milk.

Add the flours and cornstarch, baking powder, baking soda, and salt. Gradually add the chocolate chips while you stir the dry ingredients and incorporate them into the wet to make a dough.

Chill the dough in the bowl for a half hour. On a parchment-lined baking sheet, place tablespoon-sized portions of dough 2 inches apart because they will spread a lot. Flatten slightly, bake for 12 minutes, then cool on a wire rack.

Wholesome Date Oat Bars

Makes about 12–15 bars, depending on how you cut them

These bars are easy, healthy, and very versatile! They're great for a hot day when you don't feel like turning on the oven. They can even be made raw if you replace the oats with more nuts and seeds and use vanilla bean instead of extract.

12 dates (or amount that yields ½ cup of date goo)
2 tablespoons nut butter, such as almond, cashew, or sunflower
1 tablespoon agave nectar
½ teaspoon vanilla extract
1 ½ cups oats
½ cup your choice of nuts and/or seeds
¼ cup flaked coconut, sweetened or unsweetened
¼ cup raisins or other dried fruit

In a food processor, puree the dates. Add the nut butter, agave, and vanilla, and pulse until incorporated into the date goo. Pour in the oats, nuts/seeds, coconut, and dried fruit, and process until everything's chopped up small and the entire mixture forms a ball.

Press the "dough" in a shallow plastic container (more than one if needed), chill, and cut in whatever shapes you like!

Nostalgia: Everyone's Favorite Cookies

This chapter is all about the classics. No frills, just home-style cookies that are guaranteed to give you the warm fuzzies. Plus, it has five different chocolate chip cookie recipes to satisfy everyone's unique tastes.

Bakery-Style Crispy Chewy Chocolate Chip Cookies (with a Hint of Maple)

Makes about 12 large or 25 normal-sized cookies

Make these cookies BIG like those giant cookies you can find at bakeries. As their name suggests, these cookies have a chewy center contained within perfectly crispy edges. The maple syrup adds a little something, though the flavor is very subtle. The key to getting the chips evenly distributed and stuck in the dough is to use your hands!

⅔ cup canola oil
¾ cup sugar
¼ cup maple syrup

2 tablespoons applesauce
1 teaspoon vanilla extract
2 ½ cups flour

1 teaspoon baking soda
¼ teaspoon salt
¾ cup chocolate chips

Preheat oven to 375°F.

Stir together the oil, sugar, syrup, applesauce, and vanilla in a medium bowl.

Add flour, baking soda, and salt (no need to sift). Stir in chocolate chips. If the chips don't want to stick to the batter, use your hands! If the dough is a little dry, gradually add a small amount of soy milk, maybe a couple teaspoons, until it holds together.

Drop by large spoonfuls, 3–4 tablespoons each, onto a cookie sheet and slightly flatten. Bake for about 10 minutes or until the edges are golden brown.

White Chocolate Macadamia Variation: Replace the chocolate chips with ½ cup white chocolate chips (can be found all over the Internet) and ⅔ cup chopped macadamia nuts.

Kelly's Chocolate Chip Cookies

Makes about 16 cookies

This cookie recipe is veganized from the one I grew up making with my mom. It took lots of experimentation to duplicate the taste and texture. It may not be the exact recipe we always used, but I find it more than satisfactory. Its airy texture is a slight departure from your average chocolate chip cookie.

2 teaspoons cornstarch
⅓ cup soy milk
½ cup margarine
¾ cup sugar
1 teaspoon vanilla extract

1 tablespoon soy milk
1 teaspoon baking soda
2 ¼ cups flour
½ cup chocolate chips

Preheat oven to 350°F.

Dissolve the cornstarch in the soy milk and heat in the microwave or on the stove top until thickened to a soy yogurt consistency. Chill in the refrigerator until cooled, stirring every few minutes to prevent lumps.

Cream the margarine and sugar with an electric mixer. Add the vanilla, soy milk, and cooled soy milk/cornstarch mixture and combine.

Add the baking soda and gradually pour in the flour (unsifted) and mix until just combined. Stir in the chocolate chips until evenly incorporated.

Chill batter in the refrigerator for 10 minutes.

Drop by spoonfuls onto a parchment-lined or lightly greased cookie sheet, then bake for about 10 minutes or until golden on the bottoms. Cool on a wire rack, then enjoy as much as I do!

Crispy Chocolate Chip Cookies

Makes about 2 dozen

These chocolate chip cookies have a unique, shortbreadlike texture.

¾ cup margarine
¾ cup powdered sugar
¼ cup sugar
1 teaspoon vanilla extract
2 cups flour
¼ teaspoon salt
½ cup chocolate chips

Preheat oven to 325°F.

Using electric beaters, cream the margarine, powdered sugar, sugar, and vanilla together.

Sift in the flour and salt and stir until combined. Add the chocolate chips until evenly incorporated.

Flatten thinly on a greased or parchment-lined baking sheet and bake for 8–10 minutes until golden.

Soft Baked Chocolate Chip Cookies

Makes 32 cookies

These cookies will satisfy the desires of those seeking a soft, chewy, and very sweet cookie. Don't worry if they seem undercooked right out of the oven. The texture will improve as they cool and even more so overnight.

½ cup canola oil
1 cup sugar
½ teaspoon blackstrap molasses
¼ cup maple syrup or 3 tablespoons light agave nectar

1 teaspoon vanilla extract
⅓ cup applesauce
2 ¼ cups flour
1 teaspoon baking soda
⅛ teaspoon salt
⅔ cup chocolate chips

Preheat oven to 350°F.

In a medium-large bowl, mix the oil, sugar, molasses, syrup, vanilla, and applesauce. Stir.

Sift in the flour, baking soda, and salt. Gradually add the chocolate chips as you stir the dry ingredients until everything is well mixed.

Drop tablespoonfuls onto a parchment-lined or lightly oiled cookie sheet, flatten slightly, and bake for about 10 minutes or until the edges are golden brown. Remove from oven and transfer to a wire rack to cool.

Garrick's Chocolate Chip Cookies

Makes 2–3 dozen

Garrick contributed a few recipes to this book, including this one. These cookies are featured in the first issue of my friend Katie's cookzine, Don't Eat Off the Sidewalk!, and this is an updated version of the recipe. They have a thin, crispy texture and a rich buttery flavor just like bakery cookies.

1 cup softened margarine
¾ cup sugar
¾ cup brown sugar
1 teaspoon vanilla extract
2 tablespoons applesauce

2 ¼ cups unsifted all-purpose flour
1 teaspoon baking soda
1 teaspoon salt
¾ cup chocolate chips

Preheat oven to 375°F.

In a large bowl, cream together margarine, sugar, brown sugar, vanilla, and applesauce until it has a somewhat smooth texture.

In a small bowl, mix together flour, baking soda, and salt. Slowly add flour mixture in and mix until smooth and thick. Stir in chocolate chips.

The dough should be more like a thick batter, and when you spoon it onto the cookie sheet (I use parchment paper) the cookies will already be pretty flat.

Bake for about 7 minutes. They should still look slightly doughy in the center when you take them out. As you let them cool, they will solidify into a toffeelike crispy/chewy texture.

DITCH THE EGGS AND BUTTER: VEGANIZING OMNIVORE RECIPES

The world of cookies is so vast, I could not possibly include a recipe for everything. However, you can equip yourself with the knowledge to turn omnivore recipes vegan, whether they be old family cookies or something you found in another cookbook.

The Butter, Lard, or Shortening: This is an easy one. You can directly substitute Earth Balance (or another vegan brand) margarine for butter in your recipe. If it calls for unsalted butter, decrease the amount of salt in the recipe, because margarine is usually salted.

Another option is using canola oil. Replace butter with two-thirds the amount of oil, then decrease any liquid in the recipe. This also works for substituting margarine with oil.

Shortening can be directly replaced with nonhydrogenated vegetable shortening, like Spectrum or Earth Balance.

For help deciding which to use and a more in-depth analysis of margarine and oil, check out page 110.

The Eggs: There are multiple ways to substitute eggs in cookies. One way is just leaving them out, but this works best if the cookies don't heavily rely on eggs for structure.

My personal favorite way to cut out the eggs is by making a soy milk/cornstarch concoction. Dissolve a tablespoon of cornstarch in ½ cup soy milk and heat in the microwave (15-second intervals, stirring in between) or on the stove over medium heat until thickened. Let cool. This replaces two eggs. Add a splash of vinegar to this and it becomes a substitution for plain yogurt!

One-fourth cup applesauce is the equivalent of one egg, but be aware that it might make the final product a bit cakelike.

One-fourth cup soy yogurt (or makeshift soy yogurt) is the equivalent of one egg.

One tablespoon ground flaxseeds whisked together with 3 tablespoons water or soy milk replaces one egg and adds fiber to your baked goods!

If your recipe relies on multiple eggs for structure and binding, consider using plain mashed potatoes, ¼ cup per egg, as a substitute. The thickness is important when a recipe contains eggs for more than just moisture and some binding.

I usually don't like using tofu in baked goods because I swear I can taste it and it contributes to the stereotype that vegans throw tofu in everything they make. But if you'd like to use it as an egg replacer, ¼ cup blended silken tofu is the equivalent of one egg.

There are also commercial powdered egg replacers on the market that you mix with water and add to a recipe, but I'm not a fan because they can add a chalky aftertaste—and it feels like cheating.

The Milk or Buttermilk: Cow's milk can of course be directly replaced by soy milk, rice milk, almond milk, oat milk, hazelnut milk, hemp milk, or any other kind of vegan milk you can find.

For a buttermilk replacement, add a teaspoon of apple cider vinegar to a cup of soy milk and let sit for 5 minutes.

Honey: Agave nectar tastes very similar to honey and can be used as a direct substitution.

Amazingly Soft Sugar Cookies

Makes about 2 dozen or more, depending on size

This basic sugar cookie recipe was veganized from a family recipe for Christmas cookies, but it is great to use for all sorts of occasions.

½ cup soy milk plus 1 tablespoon cornstarch, dissolved
¾ cup margarine
1 ¼ cups sugar
3 tablespoons agave nectar or other liquid sugar

1 teaspoon vanilla extract
¼ cup soy milk, plus more as needed
4 cups flour
1 tablespoon baking powder
⅛ teaspoon salt

Heat the soy milk/cornstarch mixture either on the stove top or in the microwave, until thick. Set aside to cool.

Cream margarine, sugar, and agave with an electric mixer or a very strong fork. Add cooled soy milk mixture and vanilla. Add ¼ cup soy milk. Sift in the flour, baking powder, and salt, a little at a time, mixing as you go. Add more soy milk if dough is too dry.

Refrigerate for about an hour or up to overnight. Alternatively, you can freeze the dough for about 15 minutes if you're in a hurry.

Preheat oven to 350°F.

Lightly flour a countertop and rolling pin. Roll out a portion of the dough to about ¼-inch thick. Using cookie cutters, cut out shapes and place them on a cookie sheet that has been lightly misted with oil. Bake for about 5–7 minutes (again, my oven bakes things oddly, so you may want to note how long they take for you), until slightly golden on the bottom, but still soft to the touch. Cool on racks and decorate however you please (see tips on decorating cookies on page 266 and frosting and sprinkles recipes). I usually decorate with frosting and sprinkles or other little candies.

Variations: Add 1 teaspoon strawberry or other fruit-flavored extract to the dough.

Add food coloring when you add the vanilla extract.

Break the dough in half and knead in two different food colors before chilling. Either roll out separately or squish them together for a tie-dye pattern.

Amazingly Soft Chocolate Sugar Cookies

*Makes about
2 dozen
or more,
depending on
size*

These basic chocolate sugar cookies are ready for decorations or delicious on their own.

½ cup soy milk (chocolate if you have
   it) plus 1 tablespoon cornstarch,
   dissolved
¾ cup margarine
1 cup sugar
3 tablespoons agave nectar

¼ cup soy milk plus more as needed
1 teaspoon vanilla extract
3 ⅓ cups flour
⅔ cup cocoa powder
1 tablespoon baking powder
⅛ teaspoon salt

Heat the soy milk/cornstarch mixture either on the stove top or in the microwave until thick. Set aside to cool. Cream margarine, sugar, and agave with an electric mixer or a very strong fork. Add cooled soy milk mixture and vanilla. Add ¼ cup soy milk. Sift in the flour, cocoa, baking powder, and salt, a little at a time, mixing as you go. Add more soy milk if dough is too dry. Refrigerate for about an hour or up to overnight. Alternatively, you can freeze the dough for about 15 minutes if you're in a hurry.

Preheat oven to 350°F.

Lightly flour a countertop and rolling pin. Roll out a portion of the dough to about ¼-inch thick. Using cookie cutters, cut out shapes and place them on a cookie sheet that has been lightly misted with oil. Bake for about 5–7 minutes, until the cookies are slightly golden on the bottom but still soft to the touch. Cool on racks and decorate however you please (see tips on decorating cookies on page 266 and frosting and sprinkles recipes). I usually decorate with frosting and sprinkles or other little candies.

> **Variations:** Add 1 teaspoon strawberry or other fruit-flavored extract to the dough. Add 1 teaspoon peppermint extract for minty cookies.

Crispy Chewy Oatmeal Cookies

Makes 2–3 dozen

These cookies will satisfy the cravings of those seeking a sweet, chewy oatmeal cookie with crispy edges bursting with raisins. They're the ultimate home-style oatmeal raisin cookies!

⅔ cup canola oil
⅔ cup sugar
1 cup brown sugar
1 teaspoon vanilla extract
⅓–½ cup soy milk
1 ¾ cups flour

1 teaspoon baking soda
½ teaspoon baking powder
1 ½ teaspoons cinnamon
½ teaspoon salt
2 ⅔ cups oats
1 ⅓ cups raisins

Preheat oven to 350°F.

In a large bowl, stir together the oil, sugars, and vanilla. Add the soy milk, starting with ⅓ cup (the rest will be used later if necessary). Sift in the flour, baking soda, baking powder, cinnamon, and salt. Mix until incorporated. Stir in the oats and raisins. If the dough is too dry or crumbly, add the remaining soy milk.

Taking 2-tablespoon-sized portions of dough, place on a lightly oiled cookie sheet and flatten. Bake for 10–12 minutes until golden around the edges, but don't let them burn.

Transfer to wire cooling rack.

Soft and Delicious Oatmeal Cookies

Makes about 32 cookies

I've found everyone has a different idea of what oatmeal cookie utopia is. Those of you who want a soft, lightly chewy cookie, this is it!

The best thing about oatmeal cookies is that you can add anything you want to them—combinations are endless. While they are amazing with the traditional raisins, they are also particularly dreamy with dried cranberries and chocolate chips.

⅔ cup margarine
1 cup sugar
1 teaspoon molasses
⅓ cup applesauce
1 ½ teaspoons vanilla
    extract

1 ½ cups flour
1 teaspoon baking soda
¾ teaspoon baking powder
1 teaspoon cinnamon
¼ teaspoon salt
3 cups oats

¾ cup dried fruit, nuts,
    chocolate chips, etc.
    (optional)

Preheat oven to 350° F.

Cream margarine with an electric mixer until fluffy, then add sugar and molasses. Beat for a few minutes until thoroughly mixed and very light and fluffy.

Add applesauce and vanilla and mix.

Sift flour, baking soda, baking powder, cinnamon, and salt into the wet ingredients. Beat with mixers until just combined.

Shift gears from the beaters to a simple spoon. Take a moment to lick the beaters if desired.

Add the oats and optional additions to the batter and stir until combined. Drop by spoonfuls onto a cookie sheet, greased or lined with parchment paper. Bake for about 7–8 minutes. Keep a close eye on these cookies, because they need to come out of the oven as soon as the edges start to look golden to preserve the delicious softness we love about oatmeal cookies. Transfer to a cooling rack and enjoy!

Flapjacks

Makes an 8x8-inch tray

No, not pancakes! Flapjacks in the United Kingdom are sweet chewy gooey oat bars, similar to granola bars. Here is a basic recipe. Feel free to add raisins, other dried fruits, nuts, or chocolate chips!

½ cup sugar
½ cup brown sugar
½ cup soy milk
⅓ cup brown rice or light corn syrup
3 tablespoons cornstarch

3 tablespoons water
1 teaspoon vanilla
2 tablespoons margarine
3 cups oats
⅓ cup flour

Preheat oven to 350°F.

In a small saucepan over medium heat, combine the sugars, soy milk, and syrup. Cook for 5–6 minutes until the sugar dissolves and the mixture starts to thicken a bit, but there's no need to cook it all the way to soft ball stage.

Dissolve the cornstarch in the water in a small bowl off to the side, then add to the saucepan and cook for 2–3 more minutes until thick.

Remove from heat, then add the vanilla, margarine, oats, and flour. Stir.

Transfer mixture into an 8x8-inch baking pan lined with parchment paper. Bake for 14–16 minutes until golden brown, let cool in the pan, then cut and serve!

Ginger Snaps

Makes 20 cookies

These crispy little cookies are perfect for those cold winter days—or in the summer, if you don't really like to follow "rules." Neither do I.

⅔ cup canola oil
⅔ cup brown sugar
¼ cup dark molasses
¼ cup maple syrup
2 teaspoons vinegar

2 cups flour
1 teaspoon baking soda
1 teaspoon cinnamon
2 teaspoons ground ginger
¼ teaspoon salt

Preheat oven to 350°F.

In a medium-large bowl, mix together the oil, brown sugar, molasses, maple syrup, and vinegar.

Sift in the flour, baking soda, cinnamon, ginger, and salt, then stir until combined. Add a splash of soy milk if the dough is dry or crumbly.

Take 2-teaspoon portions of dough and flatten on a lightly greased or parchment-lined cookie sheet. Bake for 12–15 minutes or until the edges are crispy and the centers are firm. Transfer to a wire cooling rack. They will crisp up as they cool.

Chewy Spiced Molasses Cookies

Makes 40 small cookies

These sophisticated but humble cookies boast a deep bold flavor full of sweetness and spice. They remind me of snowy winter days.

⅔ cup canola oil
¾ cup brown sugar
½ cup molasses
2 tablespoons spiced (or not) rum
½ teaspoon vanilla extract
3 cups flour

1 teaspoon baking soda
¼ teaspoon salt
2 teaspoons ground ginger
½ teaspoon allspice
½ teaspoon nutmeg
½ teaspoon ground cloves
About ⅓ cup of sugar, to coat

Preheat oven to 350°F.

In a large bowl, cream together oil and brown sugar. Add molasses, rum, and vanilla, and mix until well-combined.

In a separate bowl, combine flour, baking soda, salt, and spices, then add to the wet mixture. Mix until combined.

Roll generous teaspoon-sized balls of dough in sugar, then press flat (about ¼ inch) onto a parchment-lined baking sheet using the bottom of a drinking glass.

Bake for 6–8 minutes, or until the cookies are firm to the touch, then transfer to a wire cooling rack. Store when completely cool.

Snickerdoodles

*Makes about
2 dozen*

These are the ultimate friend-making cookies. I think it's the cinnamon, with its compelling qualities, that makes everything just right.

¾ cup margarine

1 ⅓ cups sugar

1 teaspoon vanilla

¼ cup soy milk

2 ½ tablespoons cornstarch

3 cups flour

1 teaspoon baking powder

¼ teaspoon salt

1 teaspoon cornstarch

1 teaspoon cinnamon

1 tablespoon cinnamon

2 tablespoons sugar

Preheat oven to 325°F.

Cream together the margarine and sugar until fluffy. Add the vanilla, soy milk, and cornstarch and mix until incorporated.

Sift in the flour, baking powder, salt, cornstarch, and teaspoon cinnamon. Stir. If the dough is too dry and crumbly, add a splash of soy milk. It shouldn't be sticky, though.

Mix the sugar and tablespoon cinnamon in a small bowl. Form the dough into 1 ½-inch balls and roll in the cinnamon-sugar mixture. Place on a lightly greased cookie sheet and flatten slightly. Bake for about 11–13 minutes until golden around the edges, but still soft on top, then transfer to a wire cooling rack.

Oatmeal Scotchies

Makes 2 or 3 dozen

Vegan butterscotch chips are difficult to find, but they do exist! It's entirely worth it to track down a bag to make these classic cookies.

⅔ cup margarine

¾ cup sugar

½ cup brown sugar

1 teaspoon vanilla extract

3 tablespoons soy milk

1 ½ cups flour

1 teaspoon baking soda

¼ teaspoon salt

3 cups oats

¾ cup butterscotch chips

Preheat oven to 350°F.

Cream the margarine and sugars in a large bowl with an electric mixer. Add the vanilla and soy milk. Combine the flour, baking soda, and salt. Sift into the margarine and sugar mixture, and mix until combined. Add the oats and butterscotch chips.

Drop by tablespoon-sized spoonfuls onto a greased cookie sheet and press down ever so slightly. Bake for about 8 minutes until golden around the edges and a bit firm. These will burn easily, so don't let your precious butterscotch chips go to waste by letting them burn.

Let sit on the cookie sheet for a minute, then transfer to wire racks to cool. Store in an airtight container.

Crispy Pinwheels with Pink Sugar

Makes about 20 cookies

At the time I started formulating cookie recipes, I was at a party and there were these crispy swirled cookies with pink sugar on the edges that really caught my eye. I decided to come up with a vegan version using shortbread. While the dough is easy to prepare, the assembly takes a little practice. Working with shortbread dough in this manner can make it a little finicky, but don't give up! The vanilla and chocolate swirls are mellow, elegant, and not-too-sweet while the pink sugar on the sides adds a funky touch, making them a favorite for grown-ups and children alike.

Vanilla Dough:
⅓ cup margarine
⅓ cup sugar
½ teaspoon vanilla extract
1 cup flour
1 tablespoon soy milk

Chocolate Dough:
⅓ cup margarine
⅓ cup sugar
½ teaspoon vanilla extract
1 tablespoon soy milk
⅓ cup cocoa powder
⅔ cup flour
2 tablespoons sugar
2–3 drops red or pink food coloring

For the vanilla dough: Cream margarine and sugar together with a strong fork or electric mixer. Add vanilla. Gradually sift in the flour. Add soy milk and stir until doughlike. If it's too dry, add a splash of soy milk.

Wrap in plastic and chill in the fridge for 15–20 minutes.

For the chocolate dough: Cream margarine and sugar together with a strong fork or electric mixer. Add vanilla and soy milk. Sift in the cocoa powder. Gradually sift in the flour. If the dough won't hold together, add a splash of soy milk.

Wrap in plastic and chill in the fridge for 15–20 minutes.

Preheat oven to 350°F.

In a small bowl, mix the sugar with the food coloring until uniformly pink.

Either on parchment or plastic wrap, roll each dough out ⅛-inch thick in the shape of a square with a rolling pin. Place one of the rolled-out doughs atop the other, depending on if you want chocolate or vanilla on the outside of the cookies (the outside should be the dough on the bottom). Roll the dough out a bit with the rolling pin to help it stick better, and trim the edges, if necessary. Don't give up if it's not easy—the chocolate dough is a wee bit difficult to work with.

Very carefully, roll the dough using the parchment or plastic to help, peeling it away as you roll, as if rolling sushi. When rolled, pinch and seal the seam. Sprinkle the pink sugar on the parchment or plastic wrap, then roll the outside of the dough until completely coated with sugar, then wrap up again. Place the roll in the freezer for five minutes.

Slice the dough into ¼-inch-thick rounds and place on a parchment-lined cookie sheet.

Bake for 15–18 minutes until firm and transfer to a wire rack for cooling. The cookies will become crispy as they cool.

Sugar-Crusted Shortbread Cookies

Makes about 30 cookies

This is a nice, basic shortbread recipe to make as is or experiment with to make a variety of different kinds. Try dipping these in chocolate or adding lemon zest to the dough. Don't let the directions intimidate you—these are actually fairly simple to make.

1 cup margarine
¾ cup powdered sugar
1 teaspoon vanilla extract

2 ¼ cups flour
¼ teaspoon salt
About ⅓ cup granulated sugar, to coat

Preheat oven to 350°F.

In a large bowl, beat the margarine with an electric mixer until smooth. Add powdered sugar, and beat until smooth. Add the vanilla and mix until an even consistency is reached. In separate bowl, stir together the flour and salt. Add to the wet mixture, and mix until well combined. The dough should be neither sticky nor dry. If it's too soft, chill in the refrigerator for about 10 minutes.

Transfer dough to a gallon-sized resealable plastic bag. Keeping the bag unzipped, use a rolling pin to flatten the dough evenly, making sure to spread it to the bottom corners, then working your way up to the open end. The dough should nearly fill the bag, and should only be about ⅛-inch thick.

Refrigerate the rolled-out dough (making sure to keep it flat) for about a half hour. You could use this time to clean your kitchen and prepare for the next step.

When the dough is nice and firm, cut the plastic bag and turn the dough onto a cutting board. Using a sharp knife, trim off any rough edges, then run your knife through the dough both ways, making about 30 2-inch squares.

Gently lift each square from the cutting board, then pat both sides on a small plate of sugar. Transfer to an ungreased baking sheet (though I use parchment paper).

To avoid them puffing up, poke each one twice with a fork, penetrating to the baking sheet. You may need to hold the surrounding dough down with your fingers, as each piece will want to stick to the fork. Bake for 9–12 minutes, until the edges are golden brown. Immediately transfer to a cooling rack to cool completely.

Four-Way Chewy Ginger Cookies

Makes about 28 cookies

Spicy chewy ginger cookies. Mouth. Now. Here are four different variations to add an explosion of flavor to the basic ginger cookie we know and love.

¾ cup brown sugar
¼ cup sugar
½ teaspoon vanilla extract
3 tablespoons dark molasses
⅓ cup canola oil
⅓ cup soy milk
1 ¾ cups flour
1 teaspoon baking soda
2 ½ teaspoons ground ginger

½ teaspoon cinnamon
For classic sugar-coated ginger cookies:
¼ cup turbinado sugar for rolling, on a plate
For crystallized ginger cookies:
⅓ cup chopped crystallized ginger
Turbinado sugar

For chocolate-covered crystallized ginger cookies:
⅓ cup whole crystallized ginger chunks
½ cup chocolate chips
1 teaspoon shortening

For chocolate-covered crystallized ginger version:

Melt the chocolate chips and shortening together. Dip crystallized ginger in the chocolate and set on parchment paper. Let the chocolate harden at room temperature, then chop it up.

Preheat oven to 350°F.

In a large bowl, stir together the sugars, vanilla, molasses, oil, and soy milk.

Sift in the flour, baking soda, ginger, and cinnamon and stir until incorporated.

For classic sugar-coated ginger cookies:
Roll cookies into tablespoon-sized balls, then roll in the turbinado sugar. Flatten on a greased cookie sheet.

For crystallized ginger cookies:
Stir the crystallized ginger into the dough and roll cookies into tablespoon-sized balls. Flatten on a greased cookie sheet and sprinkle with turbinado sugar.

For chocolate-covered crystallized ginger cookies:
Stir the chocolate-covered crystallized ginger into the dough and roll cookies into tablespoon-sized balls. Flatten on a greased cookie sheet. Bake for 13–15 minutes, then transfer to a wire rack to cool.

For ginger lemon sandwich cookies: Prepare a batch of the lemon variation of Basic Buttercream Frosting (page 267) and spread between classic sugar-coated ginger cookies.

Cookies You Would Find at a Tea Party

These cookies are the type that will make everyone go "ooh" and "ahh" and think you spent forever making them. Some of these recipes do require a bit more work than others in the book, but with practice they are surprisingly easy to make.

Apricot Foldovers

Makes 3–4 dozen

This lovely cookie recipe was donated by Tami, one of my testers. Thank you! The flavor of the cookie is delicate and complemented perfectly by the sweet apricot jam.

½ cup vegan cream cheese
½ cup margarine
1 cup flour
Apricot jam or filling

Cream together the cream cheese and margarine, then add the flour until fully incorporated.

Divide dough into two discs, wrap each in plastic, and refrigerate for an hour or so. Or if you're in a hurry, pop it in the freezer for about a half hour.

Preheat oven to 375°F.

Roll dough out ⅛-inch thick, then cut into 2-inch squares with a wavy cutter for cute edges. Place about ½ teaspoon apricot jam in the center of each square.

Dampen opposite corners of each square and fold over each side.

Place on a cookie sheet lined with parchment paper, then bake for 10–12 minutes until golden.

Transfer to a wire rack to cool.

Espresso Chocolate Chip Shortbread

Makes about 30 cookies

Coffee is so good in cookies. Your kitchen will smell like a coffee shop when you make these, I promise.

¾ cup margarine

¾ cup powdered sugar

2 tablespoons ground coffee beans

½ teaspoon vanilla extract

⅛ teaspoon almond extract

1 tablespoon maple syrup

¼ teaspoon blackstrap molasses

¼ teaspoon salt

2 cups flour

⅔ cup chocolate chips, coarsely chopped in a food processer

Cream together the margarine, powdered sugar, coffee, extracts, syrup, molasses, and salt in a large bowl with electric beaters. Gradually sift in the flour and stir after each addition. Stir in the chocolate chips until evenly incorporated.

Transfer dough to a gallon-sized resealable plastic bag. Keeping the bag unzipped, use a rolling pin to flatten the dough evenly, making sure to spread it to the bottom corners, then working your way up to the open end. The dough should nearly fill the bag, and should only be about ⅛-inch thick.

Preheat oven to 350°F.

Refrigerate the rolled-out dough (making sure to keep it flat) for about a half hour. You could use this time to clean the kitchen and prepare for the last step!

When the dough is nice and firm, cut the plastic bag and turn the dough onto a cutting board. Using a sharp knife, trim off any rough edges, then run your knife through the dough both ways, making about 30 2-inch squares. Place on a lightly oiled or parchment-lined baking sheet and bake for 12–15 minutes, or until the edges are crispy and the centers are firm, but not burned.

Cinnamon Roll Cookies

Makes about 15 cookies

With their yummy cinnamon swirls, these cookies were an instant hit among testers. They're the cookie version of sweet cinnamon buns and sure to be a crowd-pleaser.

⅓ cup margarine

⅓ cup sugar

⅓ cup brown sugar

1 teaspoon vanilla extract

¼ cup soy milk

1 ⅔ cups flour

½ teaspoon baking powder

¼ teaspoon cinnamon

⅛ teaspoon salt

1 teaspoon cinnamon

2 tablespoons sugar

Combine margarine and sugars, and beat until fluffy. Add vanilla and soy milk and mix until smooth. In separate bowl, combine flour, baking powder, cinnamon, and salt. Add to wet mixture, and mix until incorporated.

Gather and form dough into a disk shape, then cover in plastic wrap and store in the fridge to chill for about a half hour, or until it can be rolled out without coming apart.

Preheat oven to 350°F.

Roll out the dough into an 8x8-inch square, about ¼-inch thick. Trim the edges. Turn flattened dough onto a piece of plastic wrap or parchment paper. (Put a piece over the dough, grab an edge, and flip it.)

Combine the cinnamon and sugar, and sprinkle on top of dough. Pat it in and brush off the excess.

Using the plastic wrap or parchment paper as a helper, begin rolling. When the dough is all rolled up, wrap the log, put it on a plate, and stick it in the freezer for about 15 minutes.

Slice the dough into ½-inch sections, and put them onto a baking sheet lined with parchment paper. I put the rough side up (the other side will be smoother from the knife). One edge of the dough will probably be flattened due to pressure put upon it from the cutting. Pinch it into shape, but it doesn't have to be perfect. The dough will not stick to itself on the cinnamon/sugared side, but that is fine. It'll bake together and have a better cinnamon roll shape. Bake for 7–9 minutes. Leave on baking sheet for 1 minute, then transfer to cooling rack.

Carrot Cake Cookies

Makes 8–16 sandwich cookies, depending on shape and size

These lovely, chewy, and spicy carrot cookies sandwich a thick layer of vegan cream cheese icing. Make the cookies into any shape you like! Carrot-shaped cookies are really cute. You can take them to the next level by sticking some fake leaves (or real, but make sure they're not poisonous) in the "top." Bunny-shaped carrot cake cookies are adorable and you can even draw a face on them with extra icing and decorating supplies. You can also serve them atop coconut that is dyed green with food coloring, like grass. To grate the carrots, you can either use a box grater and chop up the grated carrot to make it finer, or use a food processor grating attachment and give it a few pulses with the blade.

⅓ cup finely grated carrot, packed (about 1 large or 2 small carrots)

⅓ cup canola oil

½ cup sugar

⅓ cup brown sugar

1 teaspoon vanilla extract

½ teaspoon dark molasses

3 tablespoons powdered sugar

½ teaspoon ground flaxseed

1 teaspoon soy milk

1 ½ cups flour

½ teaspoon baking soda

¼ teaspoon salt

¾ teaspoon cinnamon

¼ teaspoon ground ginger

A few sprinkles nutmeg

Icing:

3 tablespoons vegan cream cheese

1 tablespoon margarine

¼ teaspoon vanilla

1 ½ cups powdered sugar

Preheat oven to 350°F.

In a large bowl, stir together the carrot, oil, sugars, vanilla, molasses, and powdered sugar. Stir together the flaxseed and soy milk in a measuring cup you've already used, then add to the mixture.

Add the flour (unsifted), baking soda, salt, and spices, then stir the dough until fully incorporated. Add a tiny bit more flour if it's really sticky. Shape the cookie dough into whatever variety of pairs of shapes you choose (without cookie-cutter assistance this time; this isn't the right kind of dough to use with cutters!), flattening until they are ⅛- to ¼-inch thin. Bake for 7–8 minutes, or until completely firm and almost hard around the edges. Let sit on the tray for a couple minutes, then transfer to a wire rack to cool.

For the icing:

In a medium bowl, stir together the cream cheese, margarine, and vanilla until smooth, then add the powdered sugar and mix until fully incorporated. Add more powdered sugar if it's runny.

When the cookies are cool, generously frost one cookie of each pair, then place the other half on top so you have sandwich cookies. Decorate as desired, then enjoy!

Hypnosis Cookies

*Makes about
30 cookies*

These cookies are made from chocolate and basic sugar cookie doughs rolled together to make a lovely swirly pattern when cut. They're reminiscent of cookie dough tubes that you open, cut, and bake, except the doughs are totally DIY! While you won't need any hypnotic persuasion to try these cookies, the amazing taste will truly hypnotize you.

To use for both batches:

½ cup soy milk plus 1 tablespoon cornstarch, dissolved

Heat the soy milk/cornstarch mixture either on the stove top or in the microwave until thick. Set aside to cool.

Vanilla:

⅓ cup margarine

¾ cup sugar

½ tablespoons agave nectar

½ soy milk/cornstarch mixture

½ teaspoon vanilla extract

2 tablespoons soy milk, plus more as needed

2 cups flour

1 ½ teaspoons baking powder

$\frac{1}{16}$ teaspoon salt

Cream margarine, sugar, and agave with an electric mixer or a very strong fork. Add cooled soy milk mixture, vanilla, and 2 tablespoons of soy milk. Sift in the flour, baking powder, and salt, a little at a time, mixing as you go. Add more soy milk if dough is too dry and crumbly.

Refrigerate for about an hour or up to overnight. Alternatively, you can freeze the dough for about 15 minutes if you're in a hurry.

Chocolate:

⅓ cup margarine

¾ cup sugar

1 ½ tablespoons agave nectar

½ soy milk/cornstarch mixture

½ teaspoon vanilla extract

2 tablespoons soy milk, plus more as needed

1 ⅔ cups flour

⅓ cup cocoa powder

1 ½ teaspoons baking powder

$\frac{1}{16}$ teaspoon salt

Cream margarine, sugar, and agave with an electric mixer or a very strong fork. Add cooled soy milk mixture, vanilla, and 2 tablespoons of soy milk. Sift in the flour, cocoa, baking powder, and salt, a little at a time, mixing as you go.

Add more soy milk if dough is too dry and crumbly.

Refrigerate for about an hour or up to overnight. Alternatively, you can freeze the dough for about 15 minutes if you're in a hurry.

Preheat oven to 350°F.

Lightly flour a countertop and rolling pin. On two pieces of parchment, wax paper, or the plastic wrap you chilled your dough in, roll each of the doughs into, roughly, squares with 13–14-inch sides.

Carefully place the chocolate dough atop the vanilla dough and gently roll to help them stick together. Cut the edges perfectly straight. Use the scraps to make marbled cookies!

Begin to roll the dough with the aid of the parchment or plastic wrap (similar to rolling uramaki sushi). When finished rolling, seal any tears in the dough by pinching and smooth out the crease. Roll in the parchment paper or plastic wrap and place in the freezer for about 10 minutes.

Cutting the dough:

Unwrap the dough, slice into two smaller logs, then slice both logs of dough into ¼–⅓-inch rounds with either a sharp serrated knife, thin wire, dental floss, or thread. These methods make for a really clean cut. Place on a cookie sheet lined with one of the sheets of parchment you were using earlier (but NOT if you were using wax paper, unless you want melted wax all over your cookie sheet and cookies, and for your house to smell like burning plastic) or misted lightly with oil. Flatten each cookie with your palm.

Bake for 10–12 minutes, checking every so often. Remove from cookie sheet and place on wire rack to cool. Store in an airtight container at room temperature when cool. Hypnotized!

Variations: Add ½ teaspoon peppermint extract to each dough at the same time as the vanilla extract. Also add a small amount of no-taste red food dye to the vanilla portion of the dough for holiday cookies! Add 1 teaspoon strawberry or other fruit-flavored extract and the corresponding food coloring, if desired, to the vanilla portion of the dough for chocolate-strawberry hypnosis cookies!

Swirls didn't come out properly? Practice makes perfect, but you can salvage your cookies by squishing the chocolate and vanilla doughs together to make a tie dye-like pattern!

Cutesy Fruitsy Raspberry Almond Sandwich Cookies

Makes 18 sandwich cookies (36 halves)

These sandwich cookies are super cute and look very impressive! Vary the flavor of jam, if you like. The almonds could definitely be replaced with hazelnuts, too.

2 cups slivered almonds

1 cup margarine

⅔ cup sugar

⅔ cup powdered sugar

¼ teaspoon lemon or orange extract

2 tablespoons soy milk

3 cups flour

¼ teaspoon salt

⅓ cup raspberry jam

Preheat oven to 325°F.

Grind the almonds until fine in a food processor and reserve 6 tablespoons of them. In a large bowl, cream together the ground almonds (save the 6 tablespoons), margarine, sugar, powdered sugar, extract, and soy milk, until smooth.

Sift in the flour and salt and stir until combined.

Flour your countertop and roll out the dough ¼-inch thick. Cut out with 2-inch flower-shaped or circular cookie cutters, and cut a small hole in the center of *half* the cookies with a knife. Press the 6 tablespoons of ground almonds on top of the cookies with holes.

Bake for 9–10 minutes, or until golden around the edges and firm all over.

Transfer to a wire rack.

When the cookies are cool, spread a bit of raspberry jam atop the cookies with no holes, then top with the hole cookies, almond side up.

Iced Caramel Cookies

Makes about 20 cookies

These cookies are sweet and chewy/toffeelike, and the cookie itself has sufficient caramel flavor, so the icing is just a drizzle. They will seem soft and underbaked when coming out of the oven, but will set up nicely upon cooling.

½ cup margarine
1 ½ cups brown sugar
1 teaspoon vanilla extract
1 tablespoon soy milk
1 ½ cups flour
1 ½ teaspoons baking powder

¼ teaspoon salt
For the icing:
⅓ cup vanilla soy creamer or soy milk
¾ cup brown sugar
1 cup powdered sugar

Preheat oven to 350°F.

In a large bowl, cream together margarine and brown sugar. Add vanilla and soy milk, and beat thoroughly. In a medium bowl, combine flour, baking powder, and salt. Add the dry to the wet, and mix until well-incorporated. If the dough is crumbly or dry, drizzle a few teaspoons of soy milk while mixing, until it comes together.

Roll into balls and place on a baking sheet lined with parchment paper, 2–3 inches apart. They will spread (a lot). Bake for 8–11 minutes, until golden brown (they will look like they're not done, but will firm up when cooled). Let sit on baking sheet for 2–4 minutes, until they can safely be transferred to a cooling rack.

For the icing: In a medium saucepan, stir together brown sugar and creamer. Turn on the heat to medium, and stir until it just begins to boil. Remove from heat and stir in the powdered sugar. It may have an uneven consistency at first, but let it cool slightly (stirring every once in a while) before icing the cookies and it should be smooth.

Place the parchment paper you used or paper towels under the cooling rack and drizzle the cooled cookies with the icing. Let the icing set completely before storing.

Adorable Bleeding-Heart Sandwich Cookies

Makes 15–20, depending on the size of your cookie cutters

These treats are ridiculously cute with fluted edges and a heart cut out in the middle! The jam flavor can be varied as can the shape of the cookies.

Cookies:
¾ cup margarine
½ cup sugar
¼ cup powdered sugar
3–4 tablespoons soy milk
1 teaspoon maple syrup
2 cups flour

Icing:
2 tablespoons margarine
2 tablespoons shortening
1 scant cup powdered sugar
¼ teaspoon vanilla extract
About ⅓ cup strawberry or raspberry jam

Cream the margarine and sugars together with an electric mixer. Add 3 tablespoons of the soy milk and the maple syrup. Gradually sift in the flour, stirring often. Add the last tablespoon of soy milk if necessary. The dough should be kneadable, not sticky or dry. Wrap in plastic and chill in the refrigerator for 20 minutes.

In the meantime, make the icing. Using the mixer, cream together the margarine and shortening, then add the powdered sugar and vanilla. Set aside.

Preheat oven to 350°F.

Divide the dough in two. On a floured surface, roll out each portion of the dough about ¼-inch thick. If the dough is too stiff or cracks when rolled, it is too cold. Let it sit out for a few minutes, then knead it a bit and proceed. Cut out cookies with a fluted 2-inch circle cookie cutter and set on a greased or parchment paper-lined cookie sheet. Using a mini heart (or star, or whatever tiny shape you like) cookie cutter, cut out the centers of half the cookies and collect the dough. Roll it out and cut more cookies, repeating the process until dough is gone. Half your cookies should be normal, and the other half should have a heart in the center.

Bake cookies for about 10–12 minutes, keeping an eye on the heart cookies to make sure they don't burn. Remove from the oven when the edges are golden. Let cool completely on a wire rack.

Spread 1–2 teaspoons of icing on top of each plain cookie, top with a blob of jam, then place a heart cookie on top. Repeat for all cookies. Store in the fridge, then let sit out for about 10 minutes before serving.

Inside-Out Peppermint Patties

Makes about 25 cookies

The zigzag drizzle of chocolate glaze atop these cookies makes them a beautiful work of art. It is necessary to use an electric mixer when making these cookies or else they will have a stale-feeling texture.

1 cup sugar
½ cup oil
1 teaspoon vanilla
1 teaspoon peppermint extract
½ cup cocoa powder
2 tablespoons soy milk
2 cups flour
1 teaspoon baking soda

¼ teaspoon salt
About a tablespoon of soy milk
For the icing:
3 cups powdered sugar
4 tablespoons hot water
3 teaspoons vanilla
1 teaspoon peppermint extract
1 tablespoon cocoa powder

Preheat oven to 350°F.

In a large bowl, cream together the sugar and oil using an electric mixer. Add vanilla, peppermint, cocoa powder, and soy milk, and mix until the consistency is smooth. In a separate bowl, mix together the flour, baking powder, and salt. Add to the wet mixture and mix until well-incorporated. The dough will be crumbly, so add the tablespoon of soy milk a little at a time, until the dough holds together without being sticky.

Form dough into 1-inch balls, and flatten onto a baking sheet lined with parchment paper. Bake for 8–10 minutes, or until the edges are firm. Let cool on a cooling rack completely before icing.

While the cookies are cooling, prepare the icing. In a large bowl, whisk together the powdered sugar and hot water until smooth. Mix in the vanilla and peppermint, then transfer about ½ cup (this does not have to be exact!) into a separate bowl. Add

the cocoa powder to the lesser amount, and stir until smooth. If it is too stiff to use as a drizzle, add a little water. Both icings should be pretty thick and heavy, but not stiff. When you drop the cookie in the bowl of white icing, you should need to push it down in order to cover the entire top half.

When cookies have cooled completely, dip each one (upside down) into the white icing. Let the iced cookies set on a cooling rack with a paper towel underneath to catch drips. For best results, dip the cookies a second time once the first coat has set.

Drizzle the chocolate icing over the white with a fork, and let the icing set completely before storing.

Chocolate-Dipped Powdered Cream Cookies

Makes 3 dozen or so

These are absolutely decadent and melt in your mouth! This recipe makes a helluva lot and calls for quite a bit of margarine, so feel free to halve or third it. They are great dipped in chocolate or not, so you can make these either way.

1 ¾ cups margarine
1 ½ cups powdered sugar
2 teaspoons vanilla extract
2 cups flour
1 ½ cups cornstarch

¼ cup soy milk, as needed
Powdered sugar (if not using chocolate)
For chocolate dipping
1 ½ cups chocolate chips
2 tablespoons shortening

In a large bowl, cream together the margarine and powdered sugar with electric beaters. Add the vanilla, then gradually sift in the flour and cornstarch. If the dough won't hold together, add a few splashes of soy milk, up to ¼ cup. It should be the consistency of sugar cookie dough, not sticky. Wrap the dough in plastic and chill in the fridge for a half hour.

Preheat oven to 375°F.

Form the dough into 1-inch balls and place on a parchment-lined cookie sheet. Bake for 12–13 minutes until firm and the bottoms are golden brown, but don't let them burn. Sift powdered sugar over their tops (skip this step if you're dipping them in chocolate, because the chocolate won't adhere to the cookies if they're covered in powdered sugar).

Transfer to a wire cooling rack and melt the chocolate over the stove top.

Once cooled, dip half the cookie in the chocolate.

Return to the parchment paper and let cool. Enjoy!

THE NONEDIBLE COOKIES: VEGANISM ON THE WEB

With all the resources we have nowadays, it's a piece of cake to become vegan and stay vegan. The Internet hosts thousands of vegan recipes, food blogs, vegan webstores, Internet communities, and more. Here are some Web sites to get you started.

The Post Punk Kitchen (www.theppk.com)

Best-selling cookbook author Isa Chandra Moskowitz's Web site is home of the friendliest, most resourceful vegan community on the Internet. Take a look at her recipe archive, blog, and shows, too! And of course, food porn!

Vegan Essentials (www.veganessentials.com)

For tons of vegan goodies on your doorstep, check out the online store for this Milwaukee-based company!

Pangea (www.veganstore.com)

Check these guys out for all your vegan needs. Find white chocolate chips, marshmallows, and more!

Herbivore Clothing Company (www.herbivoreclothing.com)

Herbivore has tons of awesome shirts, hoodies, totes, buttons, and more! Check out their magazine, too.

VegWeb (www.vegweb.com)

VegWeb is a mecca of vegan recipes of all kinds.

The Vegan Cookie Connoisseur Blog (www.vegancookies.wordpress.com)

My little space on the Internet for tons of news and photos!

Super-Cute Turtle Cookies

Makes about 15 cookies

These cookies are a nice balance of gooey and crunchy. They have a sweet caramel flavor and cute turtle legs.

⅓ cup oil
½ cup brown sugar
½ teaspoon vanilla extract
¼ cup maple syrup
1 ½ cups flour

1 teaspoon baking powder
¼ teaspoon salt
2 tablespoons soy milk
About ½ cup halved
    pecans

For the chocolate drizzle:
¼ cup chocolate chips
1 teaspoon shortening

Preheat oven to 350°F.

In a large bowl, cream together oil and brown sugar until well-combined. Add vanilla and maple syrup, and continue to beat until the mixture has reached a very smooth consistency. Slowly add the flour, baking powder, and salt and mix until well-incorporated. The dough should be crumbly. Add the soy milk one tablespoon at a time, and continue to mix until the dough can be easily formed into balls (and not sticky).

On a baking sheet lined with parchment paper, arrange pecans so that they form the shape of a turtle: a half-pecan for the head, and a fourth-pecan for each leg.

Form a generous 1-inch ball of dough, and press it onto the pecans. Adjust the pecans, pressing them further into the dough as necessary.

Bake for 8–10 minutes, or until golden brown. They will still be pretty soft. Carefully transfer cookies to a wire cooling rack, being careful not to touch the pecans. As they cool, the cookie will become firmer, and the pecans will better adhere to the cookies. As the cookies are cooling, prepare the drizzle. Combine chocolate chips and shortening in a small plastic zip-top bag. Microwave for about a minute, or until melted, but not too hot. Snip a tiny hole in a corner, drizzle onto cooled cookies, and let firm up completely before storing.

Vanilla Sandwich Cookies

Makes 18–20 sandwich cookies

I've given you three options of fillings for these sandwich cookies, but the possibilities are limited only by your imagination and collection of extracts and food colorings! Make a batch of one kind, or many different kinds. Will it be plain vanilla, chocolate, and strawberry or pineapple with purple food coloring?

Using the amounts of filling ingredients in parentheses will yield ⅓ of a full batch, so making all three fillings in small batches will make just the right amount of filling to create a variety of sandwich cookies.

One batch of Shortbread (page 236) dough

Vanilla filling:
¾ cup (¼ cup) shortening
3 cups (1 cup) powdered sugar
¾ teaspoon (¼ teaspoon) vanilla extract

Chocolate filling:
¾ cup (¼ cup) shortening

2 ½ cups (⅔ cup plus 3 ½ tablespoons) powdered sugar
½ cup (3 ½ tablespoons) cocoa powder
¾ teaspoon (¼ teaspoon) vanilla extract

Strawberry filling:
¾ cup (¼ cup) shortening
3 cups (1 cup) powdered sugar
1 teaspoon (½ teaspoon) strawberry extract

Preheat oven to 350°F.

Prepare shortbread dough according to directions, but cut into circles (about 1 ½-inch) instead of squares. Bake for 8–10 minutes or until golden, then transfer to a wire cooling rack.

Prepare the fillings you are using by stirring all ingredients of each filling in a small bowl. When cookies are cool, put about a teaspoon of filling on one cookie, then smoosh the other half on it. Repeat for all cookies, then devour!

Decorating: Ideas and Recipes for Homemade Cookie Fixin's

The extra step of decorating will bring something special to otherwise plain cookies.

Make Your Own Sprinkles Kit

Many commercial sprinkles and candies have a seemingly vegan ingredient called confectioner's glaze added to them. However, confectioner's glaze is actually insect secretion and not vegan at all, so be sure to avoid it while browsing for decorations.

Don't worry! You can find a selection of vegan-friendly sprinkles at natural food stores and all over the Internet. Some mainstream companies do have vegan sprinkles, though. Just check the labels!

You can also make your own sugar sprinkles in a pinch by mixing granulated or coarse sugar with food coloring. Your homemade sprinkles may clump up from time to time, but you can break them up easily with a fork. I may or may not own a homemade sprinkles kit with separate compartments for a full rainbow of colors.

Basic Buttercream Frosting

Makes about 2 cups of frosting, enough to frost a batch of sugar cookies

It's basic. It's buttercream. It's delicious! Frost a batch of sugar cookies, a cookie cake, or even use as a sandwich cookie filling. It halves, doubles, triples, and quadruples well.

¼ cup vegetable shortening
¼ cup margarine
2 cups powdered sugar

2 tablespoons soy milk
1 teaspoon vanilla extract

Cream together the shortening and margarine with electric beaters or a strong fork. Add powdered sugar a little at a time, drizzling in soy milk, if necessary. Add vanilla and extracts/food coloring (if using) and beat until fluffy.

Variations: For Chocolate Buttercream, replace ½ cup of the powdered sugar with cocoa powder.

- Add ½ teaspoon strawberry or raspberry extract.
- Add 2 teaspoons lemon zest and replace half the soy milk with lemon juice.
- Add ¼ teaspoon root beer extract.
- Add a small amount of food coloring for brightly colored frosting.

Marzipan

Makes 1½ cups

Marzipan is a sweet almond paste made from blanched almonds, powdered sugar, and extracts. Many store-bought marzipans contain egg whites, so a vegan version can sometimes be hard to find and when you do, it's often obscenely expensive. Never fear, homemade marzipan is within your reach! Use your marzipan for making little shapes, fruits, or sculptures to decorate baked goods. This recipe can be doubled, halved, thirded, one-seventh-ed, etc. Homemade marzipan tends to be a little bit oily no matter what, so it's best used in recipes and for little sculptures, but may be kind of difficult for tiny details.

2 cups blanched almonds
2 teaspoons vanilla extract
2 teaspoons almond extract
1 teaspoon rosewater (optional)

2 ½–3 cups powdered sugar
1–2 tablespoons water, if necessary
Food coloring (optional)

Put the almonds into a food processor and process for about 4 minutes. Add the extracts and process for a few more minutes. It's okay if it looks dry. Add the powdered sugar little by little. You may not need all of it or you may need more, depending on the consistency of your almonds. Process for a few minutes. If your marzipan isn't holding together like dough (it's perfectly fine if it isn't), add the water, a little at a time, until it collects into a ball.

At this point, you can divide the dough and add the food colorings. This is easily achieved in the food processer.

Refrigerate your marzipan for at least 45 minutes to an hour, then enjoy!

Index

Conversion Chart

The following conversions have been rounded up or down slightly to simplify measuring.

Weight	
American	Metric
1/4 oz	7 g
1/2 oz	15 g
1 oz	30 g
2 oz	60 g
3 oz	90 g
4 oz	115 g
5 oz	150 g
6 oz	175 g
7 oz	200 g
8 oz (1/2 lb)	225 g
9 oz	250 g
10 oz	300 g
11 oz	325 g
12 oz	350 g
13 oz	375 g
14 oz	400 g
15 oz	425 g
16 oz (1 lb)	450 g
1 1/2 lb	750 g
2 lb	900 g
2 1/4 lb	1 kg
3 lb	1.4 kg
4 lb	1.8 kg

Volume		
American	Metric	Imperial
1/4 t	1.2 ml	
1/2 t	2.5 ml	
1 t	5.0 ml	
1/2 T (1.5 t)	7.5 ml	
1 T (3 t)	15 ml	
1/4 cup (4 T)	60 ml	2 fl oz
1/3 cup (5 T)	75 ml	2 1/2 fl oz
1/2 cup (8 T)	125 ml	4 fl oz
2/3 cup (10 T)	150 ml	5 fl oz
3/4 cup (12 T)	175 ml	6 fl oz
1 cup (16 T)	250 ml	8 fl oz
1 1/4 cups	300 ml	10 fl oz (1/2 pt)
1 1/2 cups	350 ml	12 fl oz
2 cups (1 pint)	500 ml	16 fl oz
2 1/2 cups	625 ml	20 fl oz (1 pint)
1 quart	1 liter	32 fl oz

Oven Temperature		
F	Gas Mark	Description
225	1/4	Very cool/very slow
250	1/2	—
275	1	cool
300	2	—
325	3	very moderate
350	4	moderate
375	5	—
400	6	moderately hot
425	7	hot
450	8	—
475	9	very hot